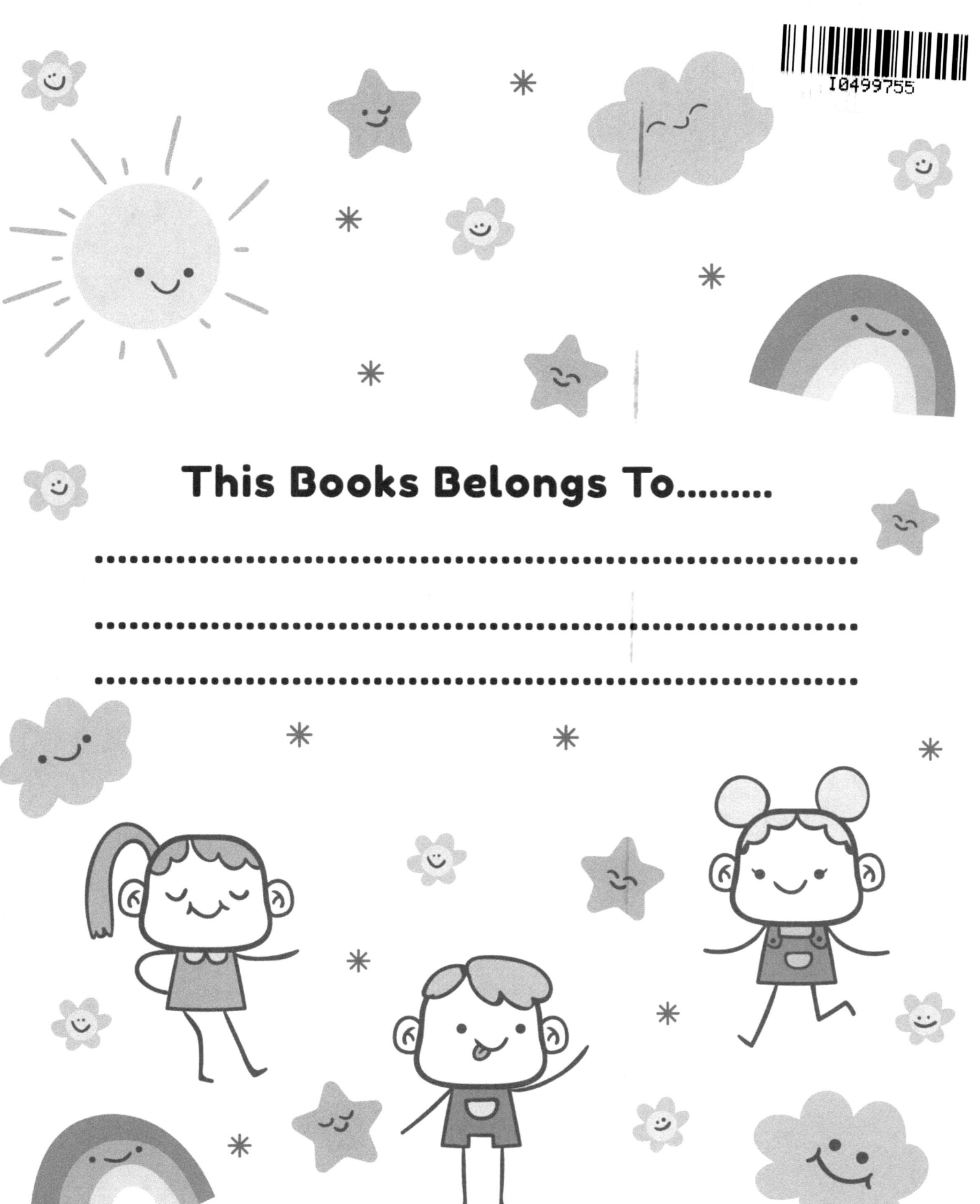

# This Books Belongs To.........

..............................................................

..............................................................

..............................................................

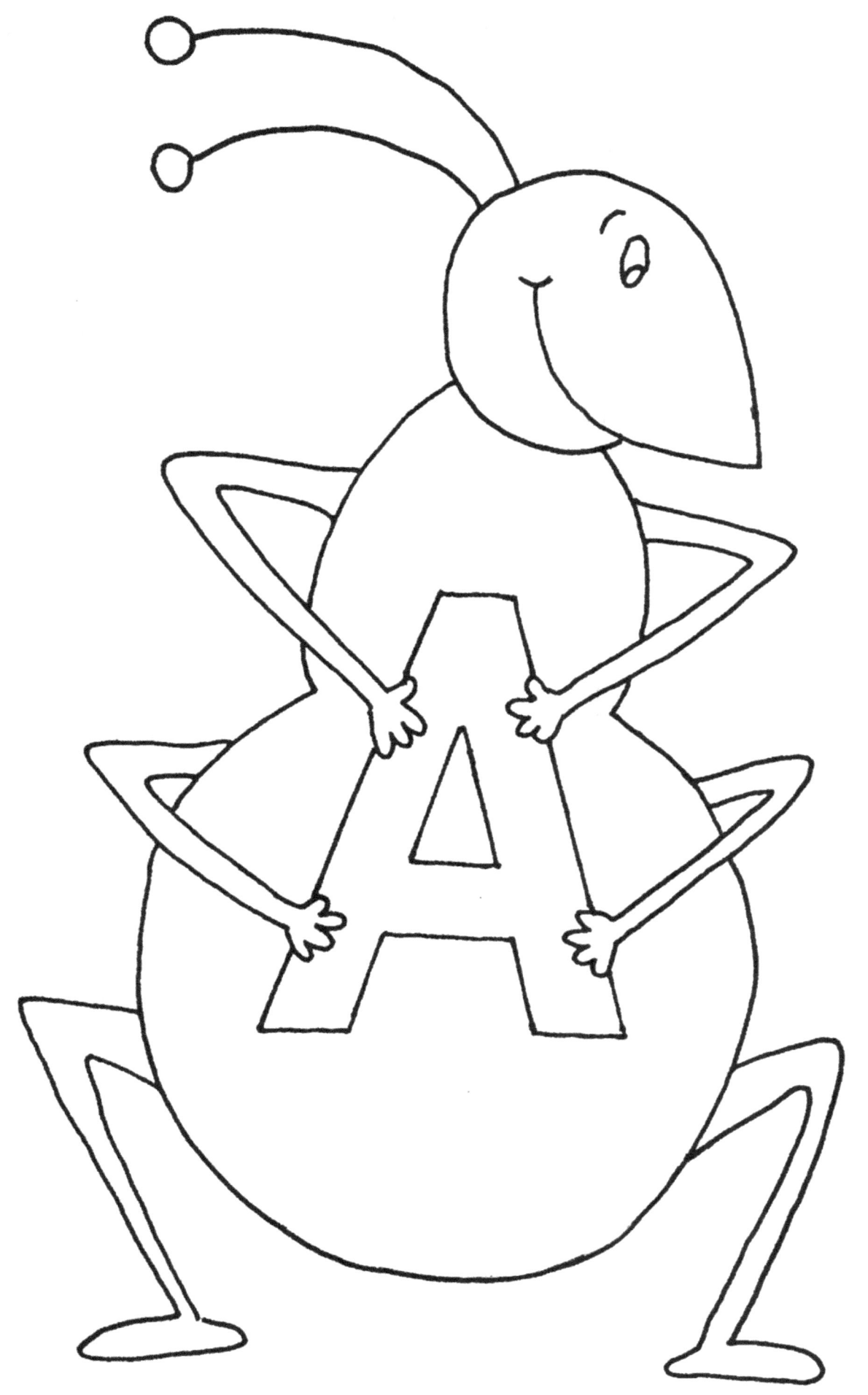

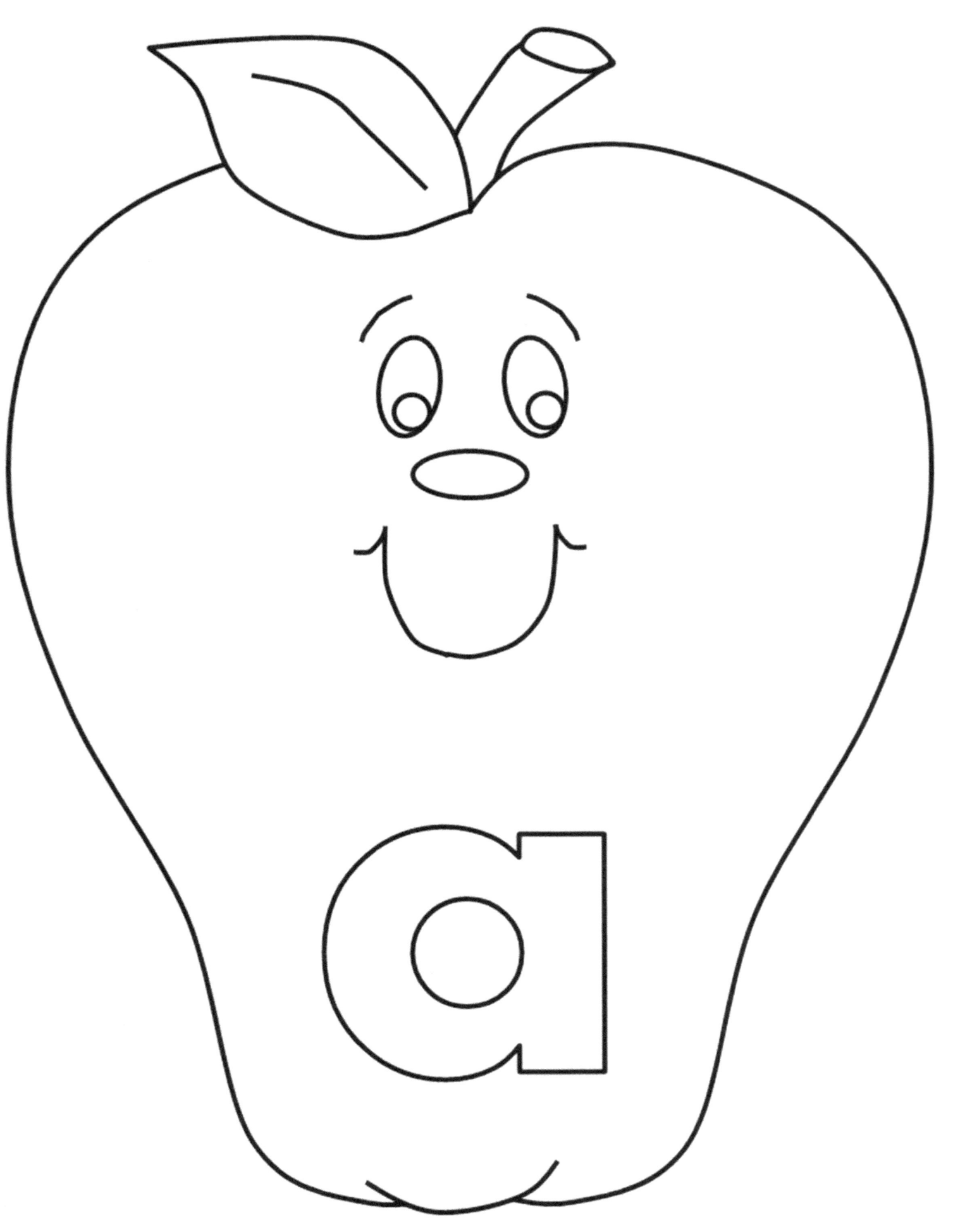

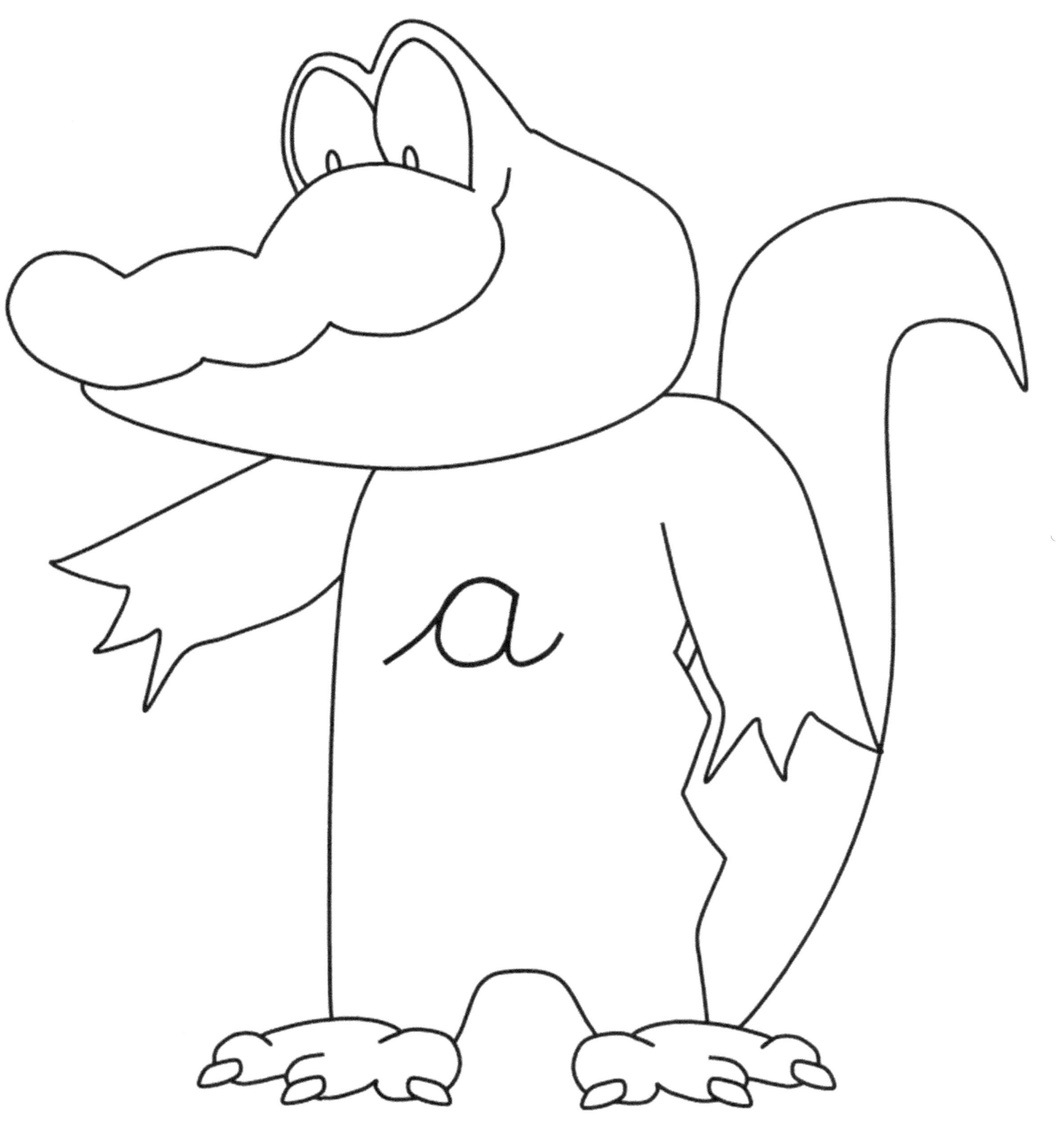

Trace the steps for making the letter a on the following line.

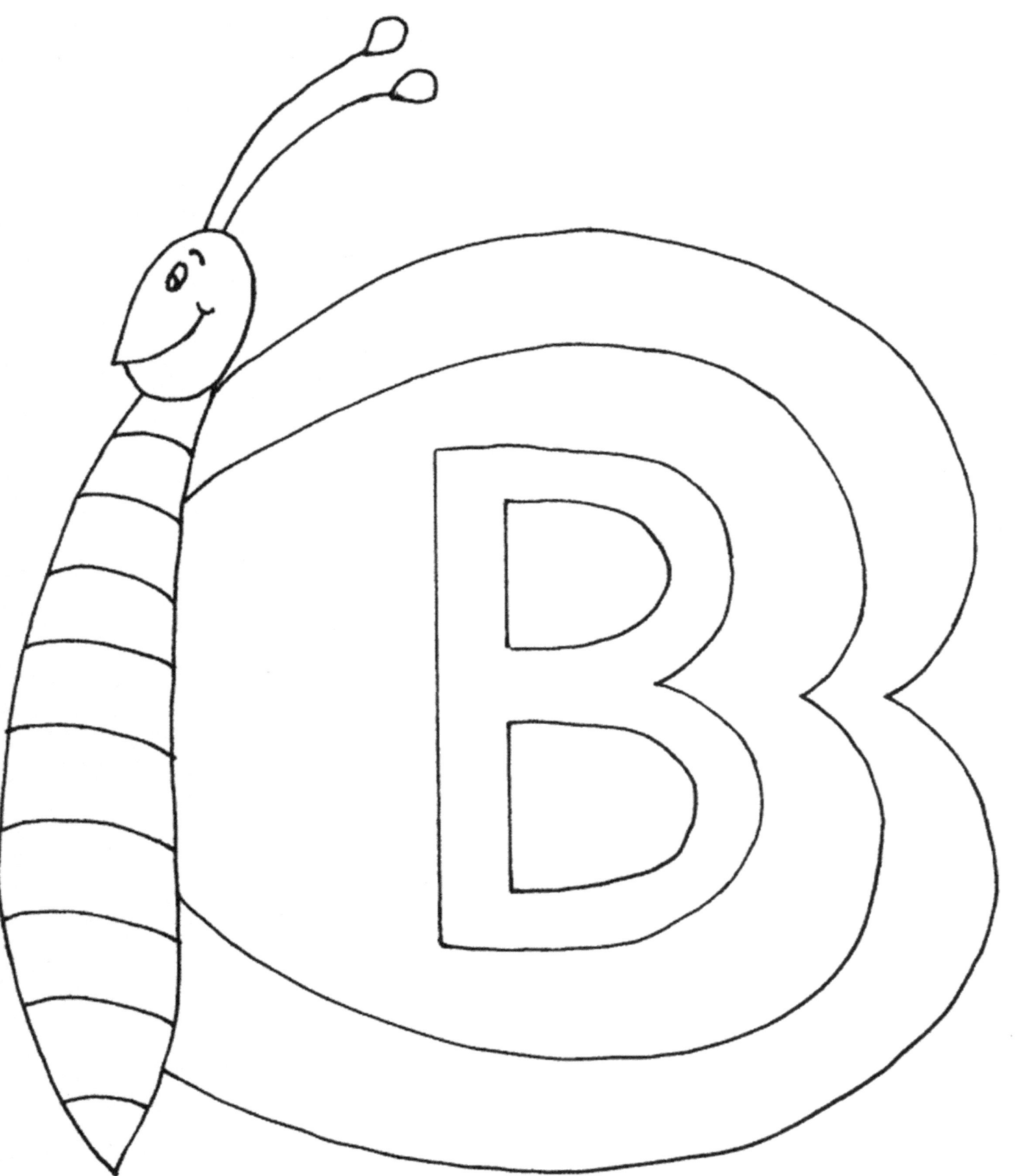

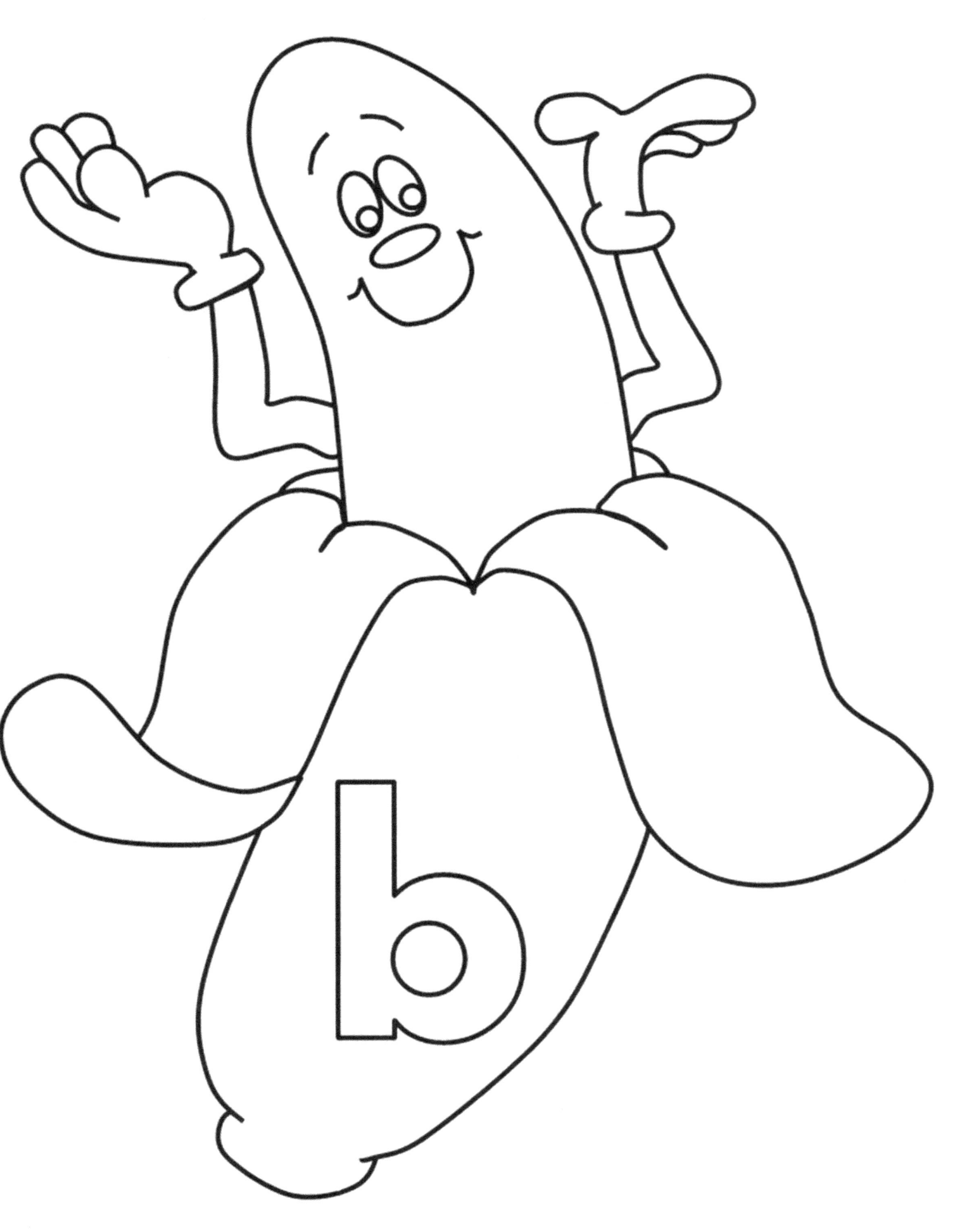

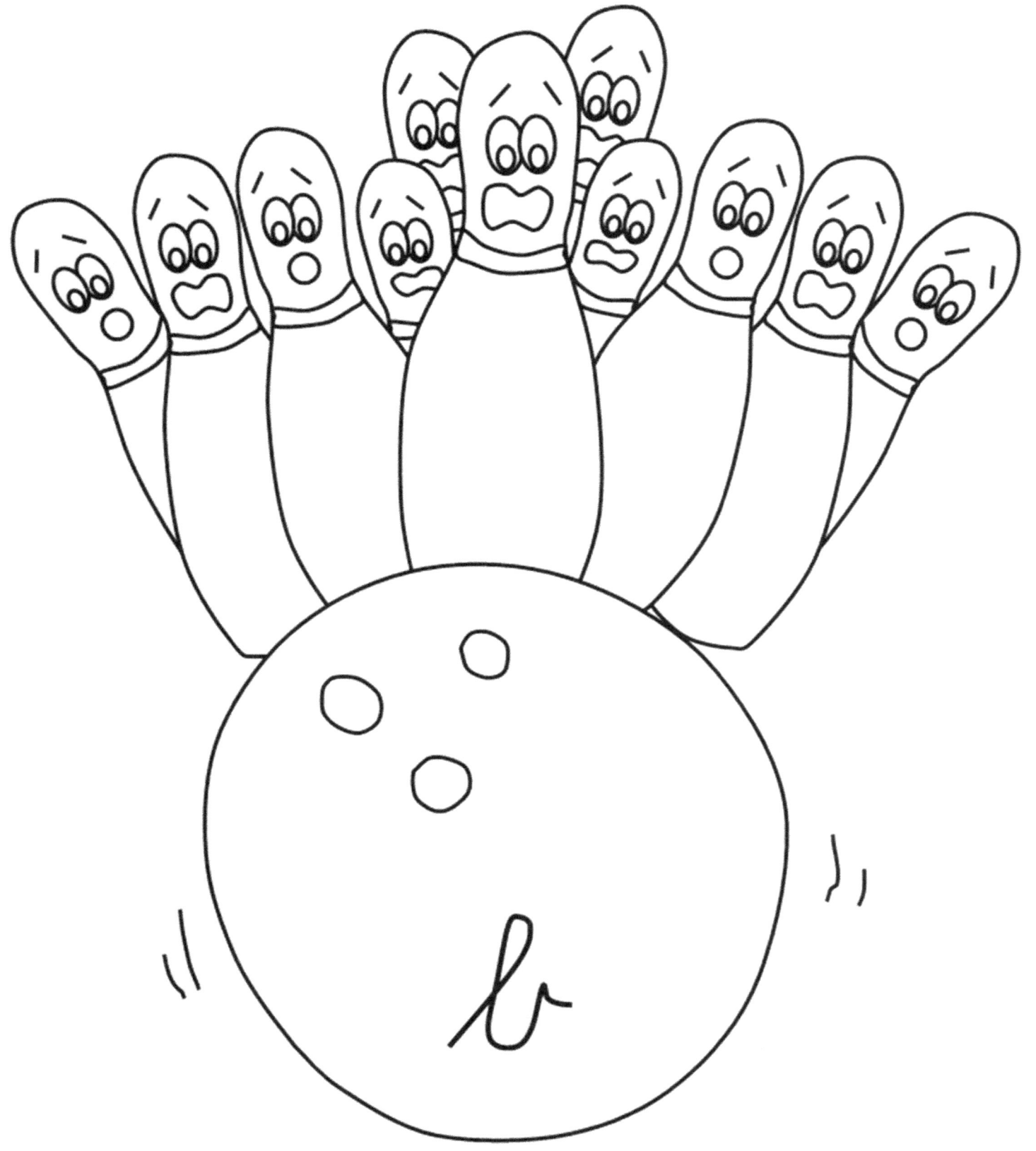

Trace the steps for making the letter b on the following line.

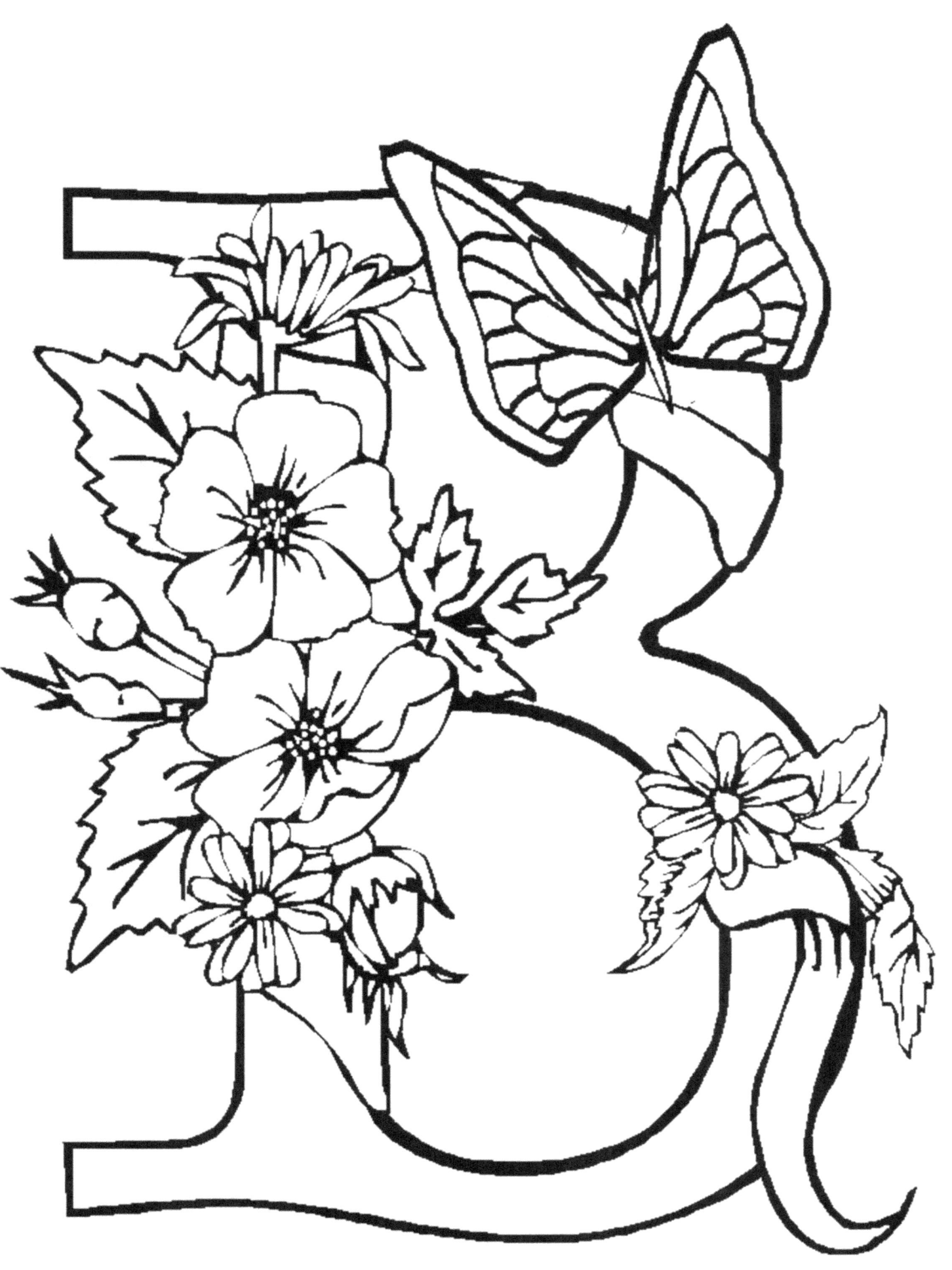

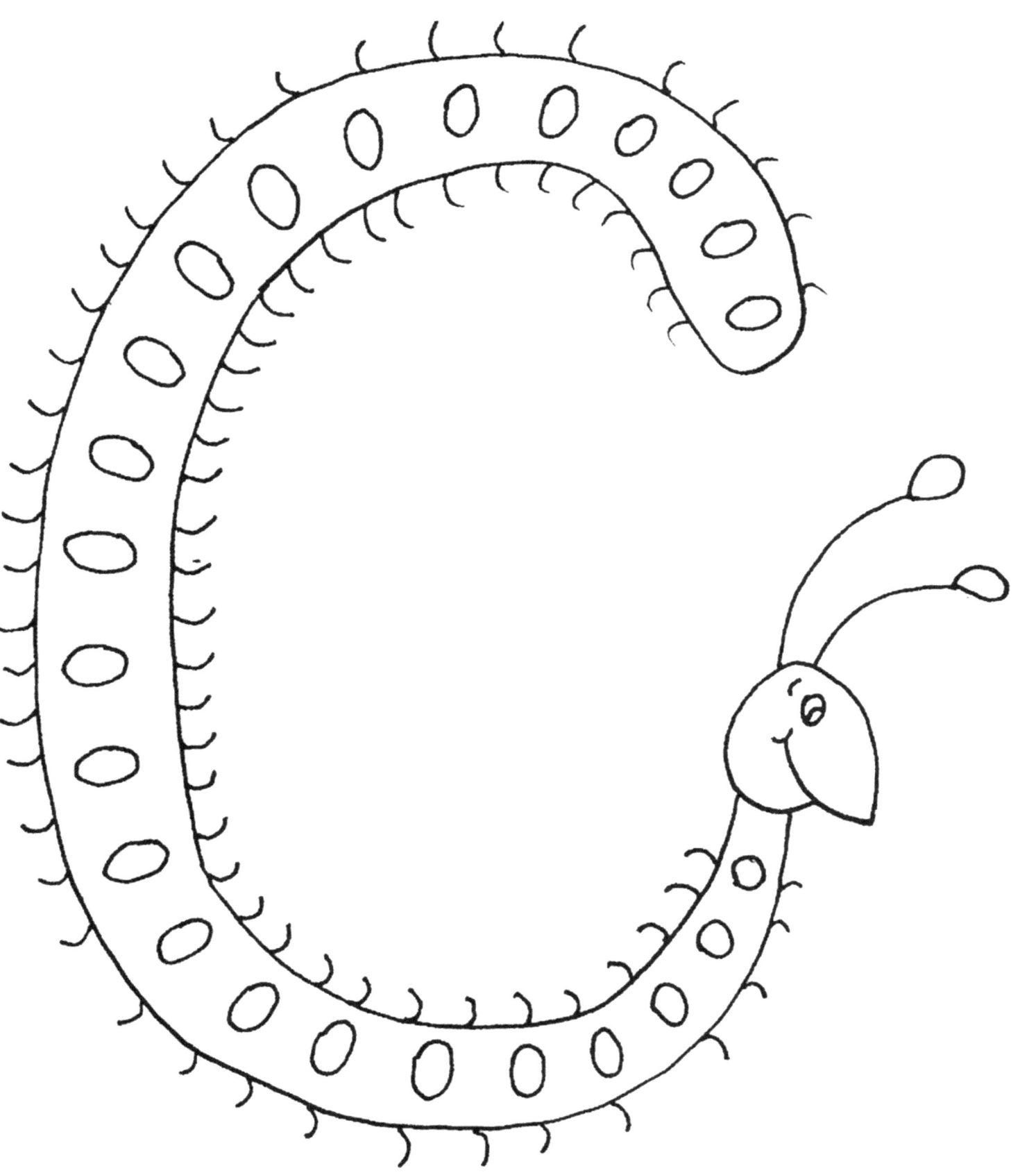

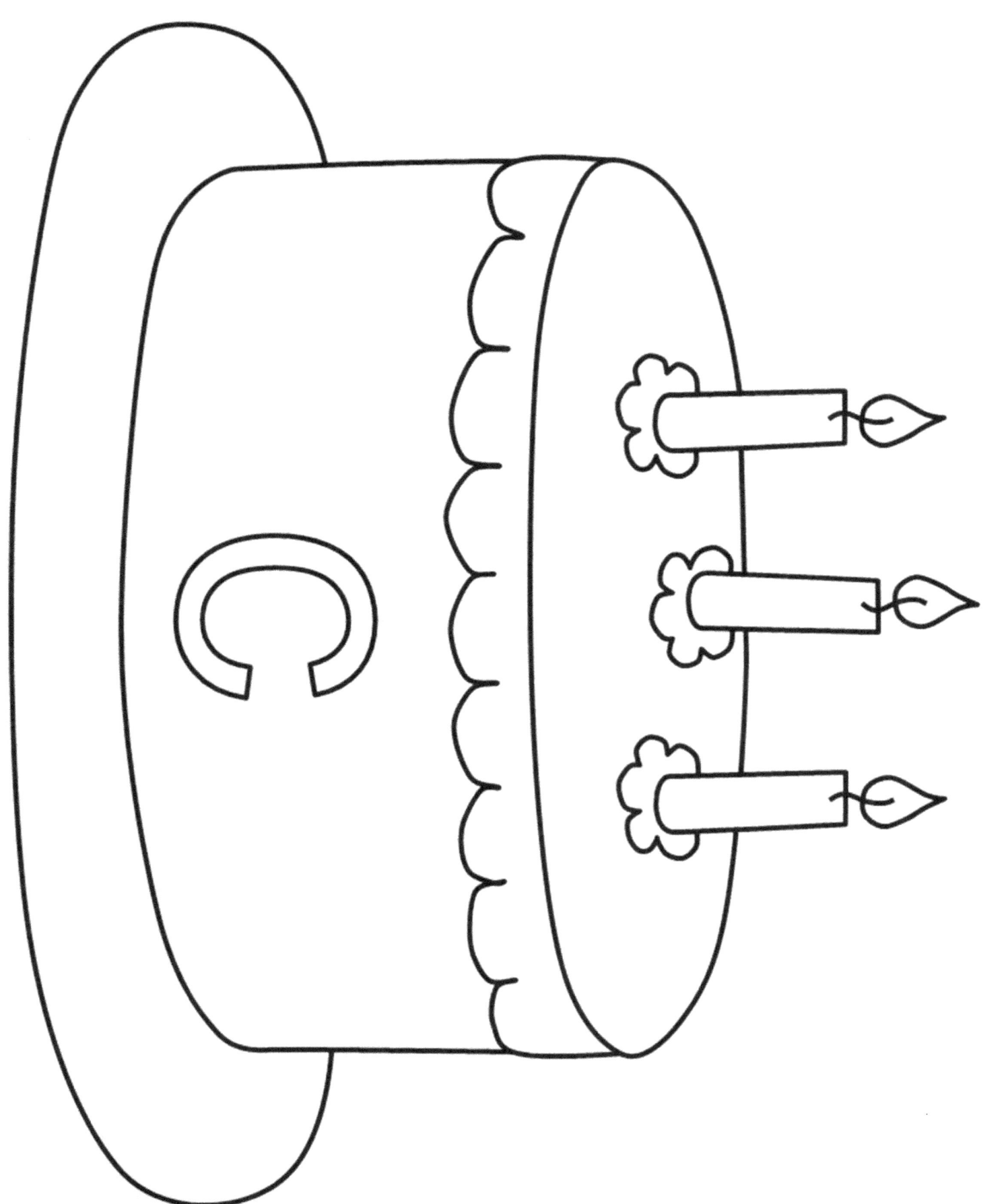

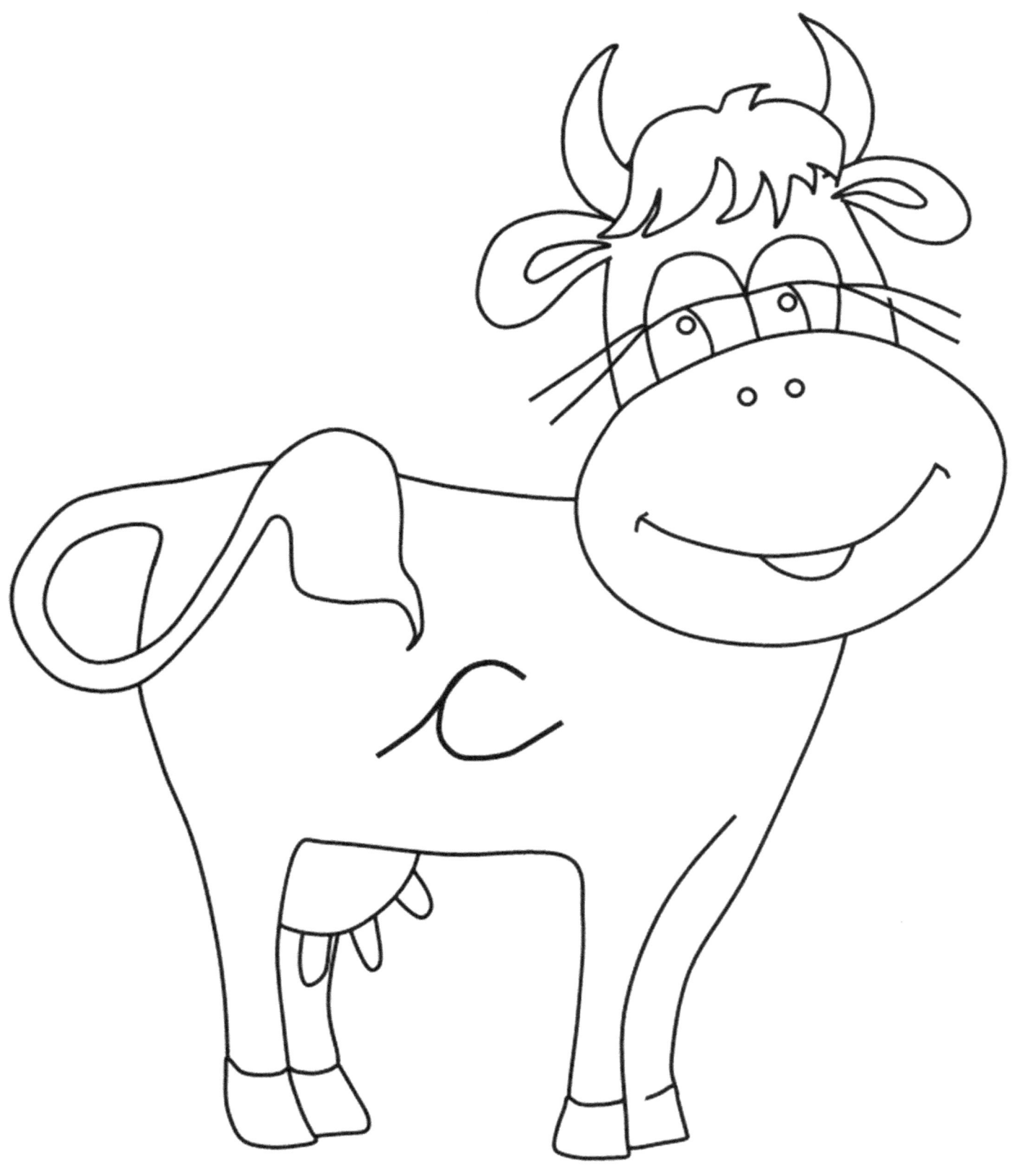

Trace the steps for making the letter c on the following line.

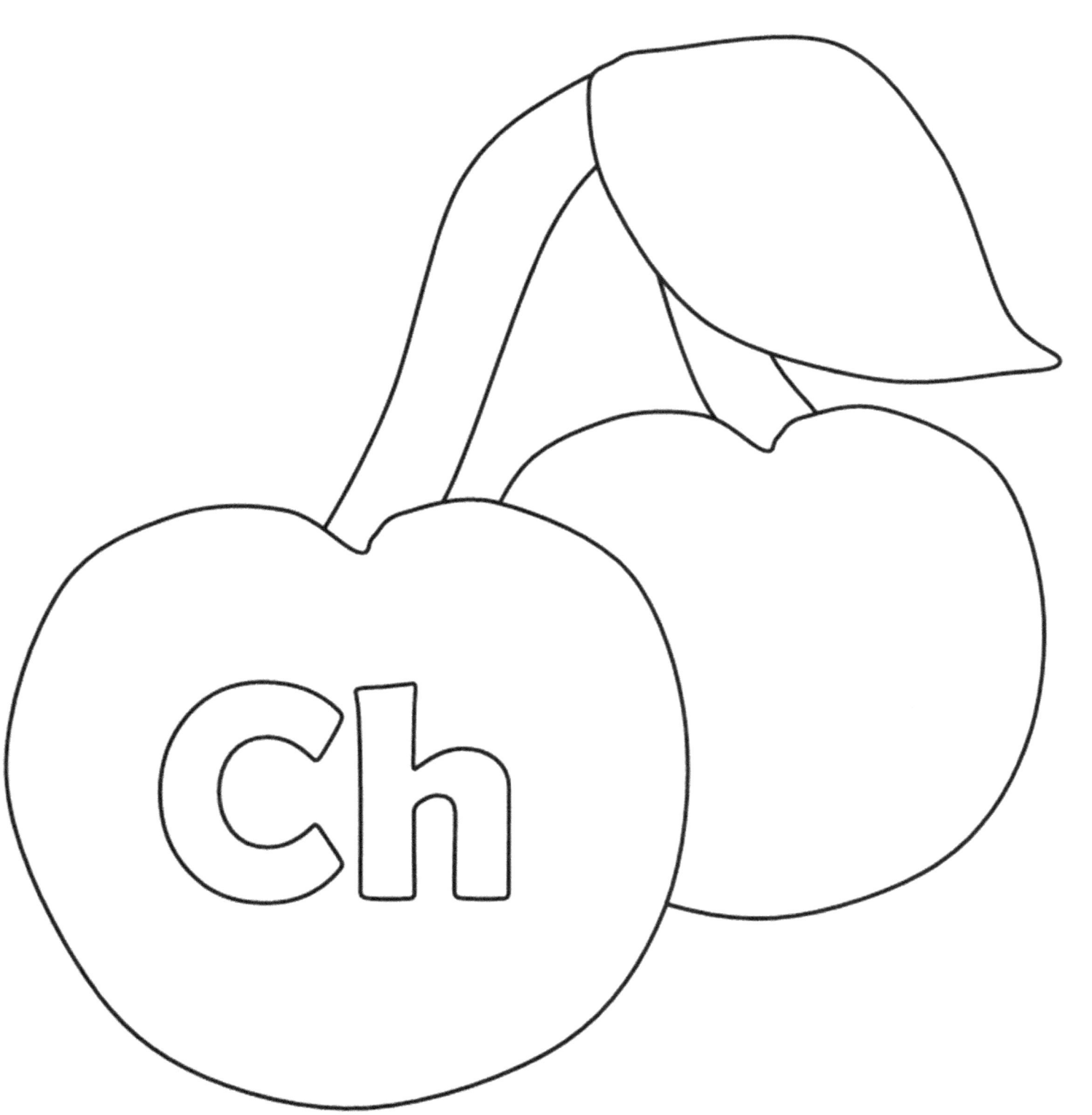

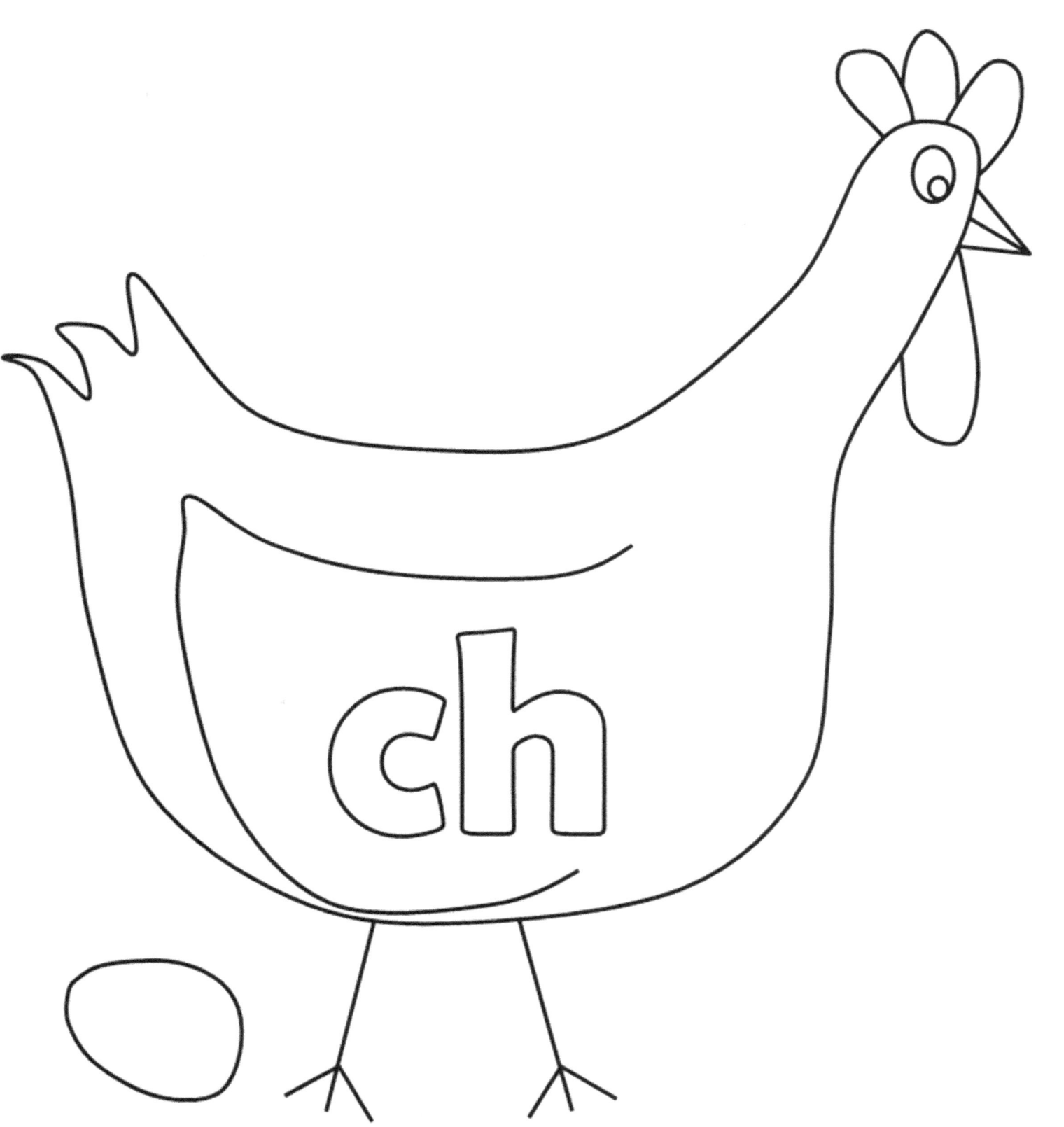

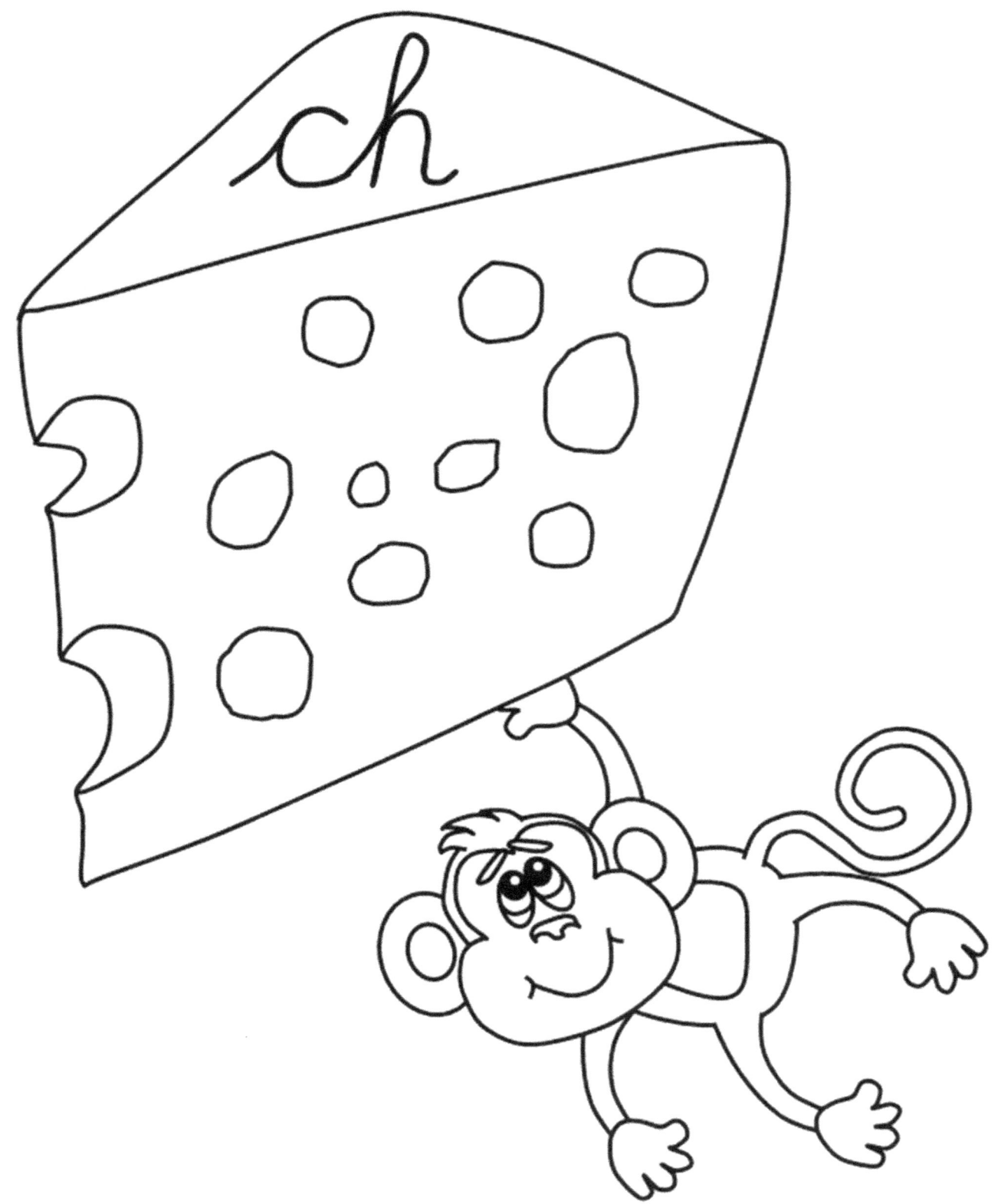

Trace the steps for making the letter c on the following line.

*c   h   ch   ch   ch   ch*

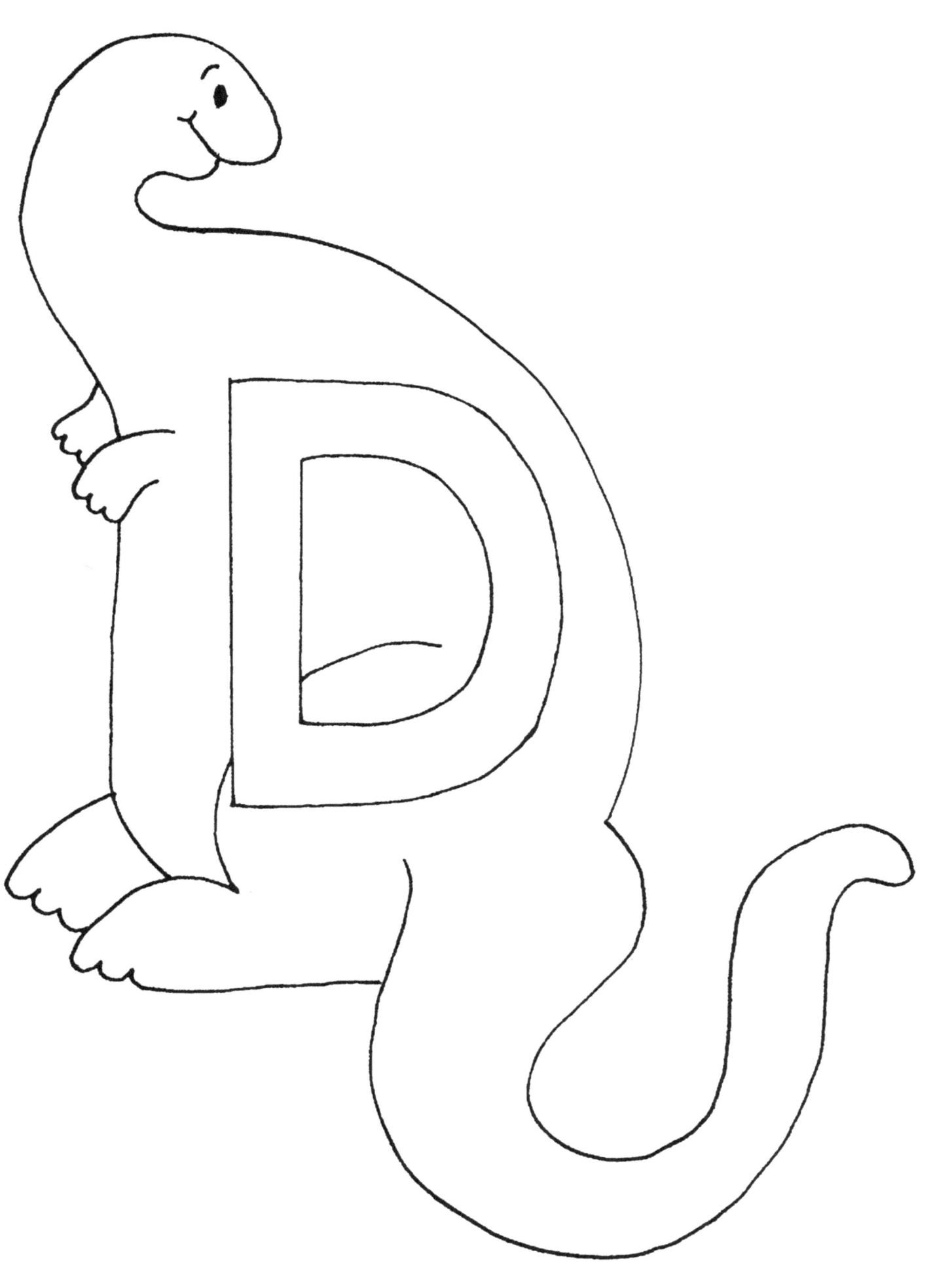

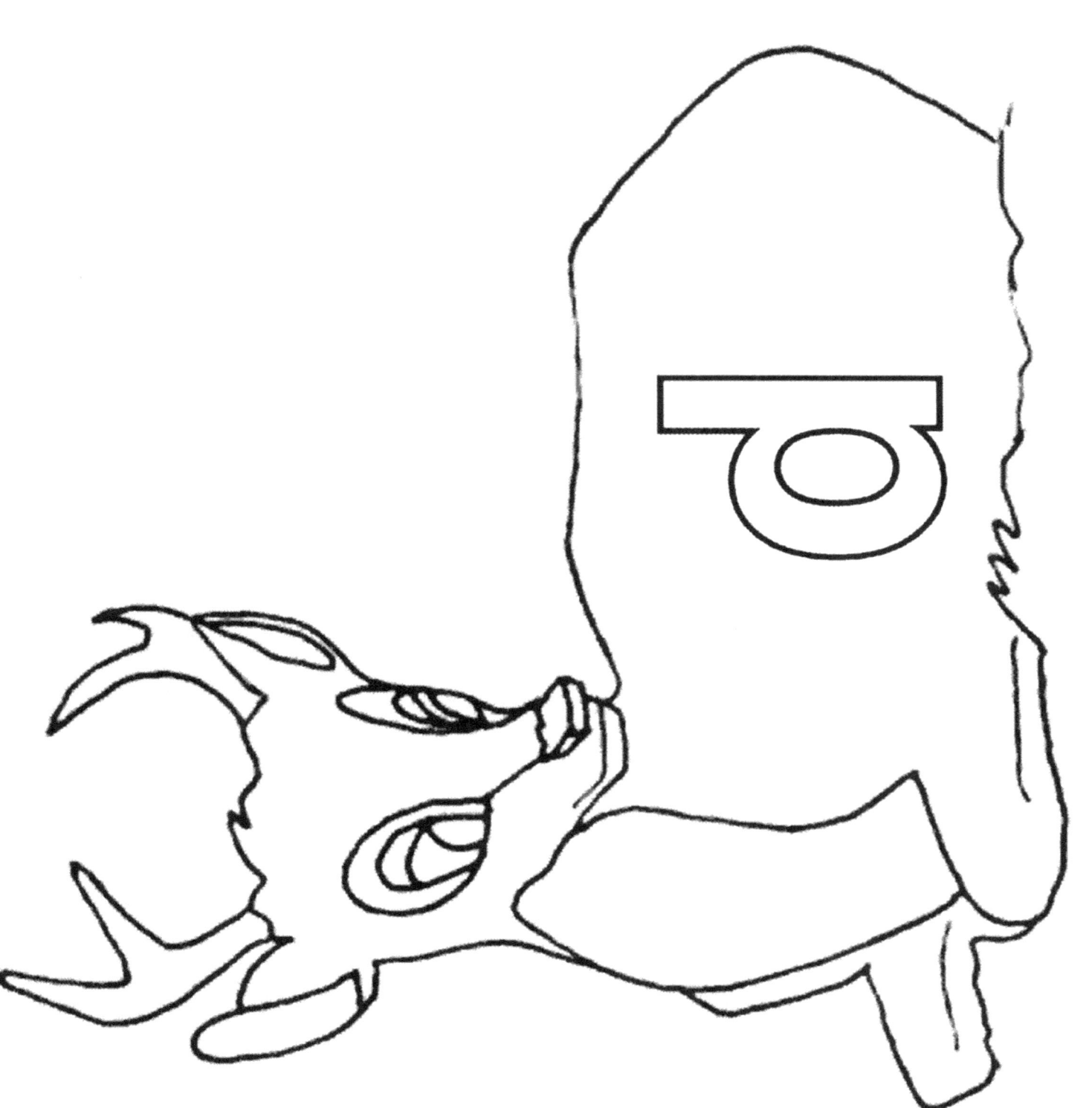

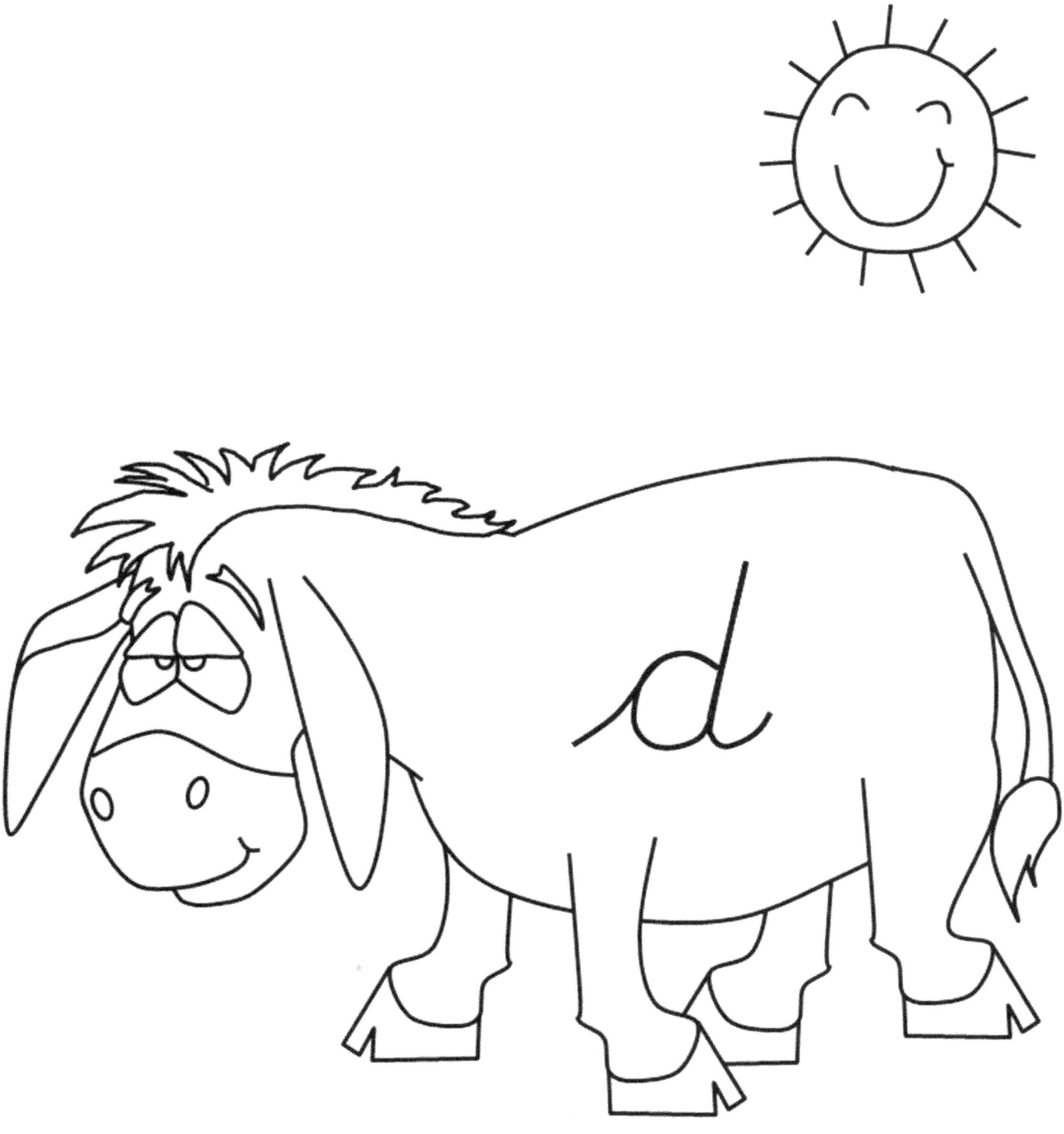

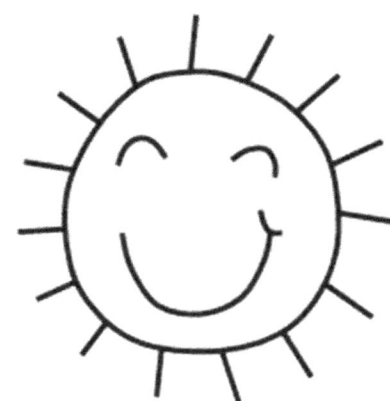

d

Trace the steps for making the letter d on the following line.

d    d    d    d    dd

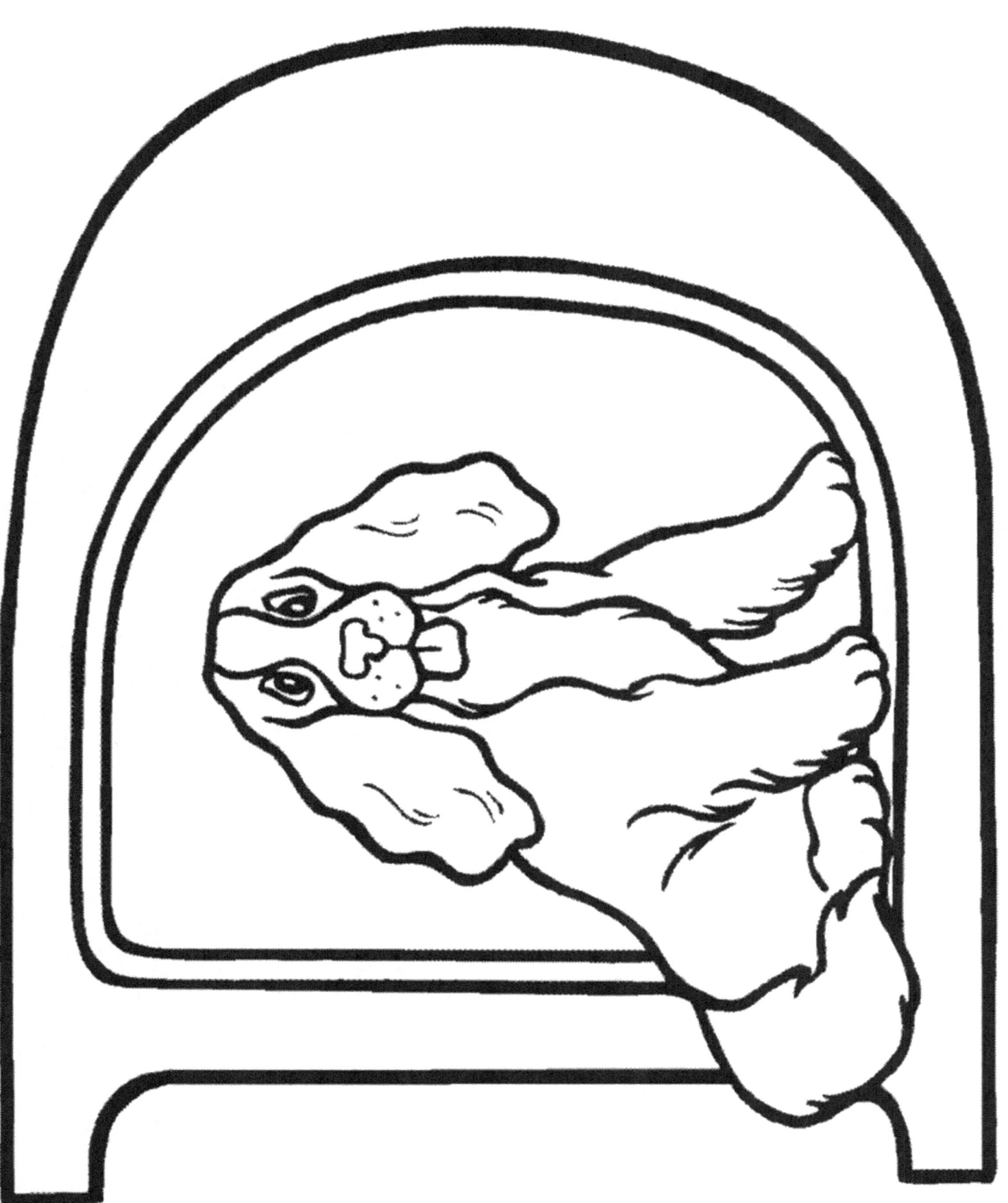

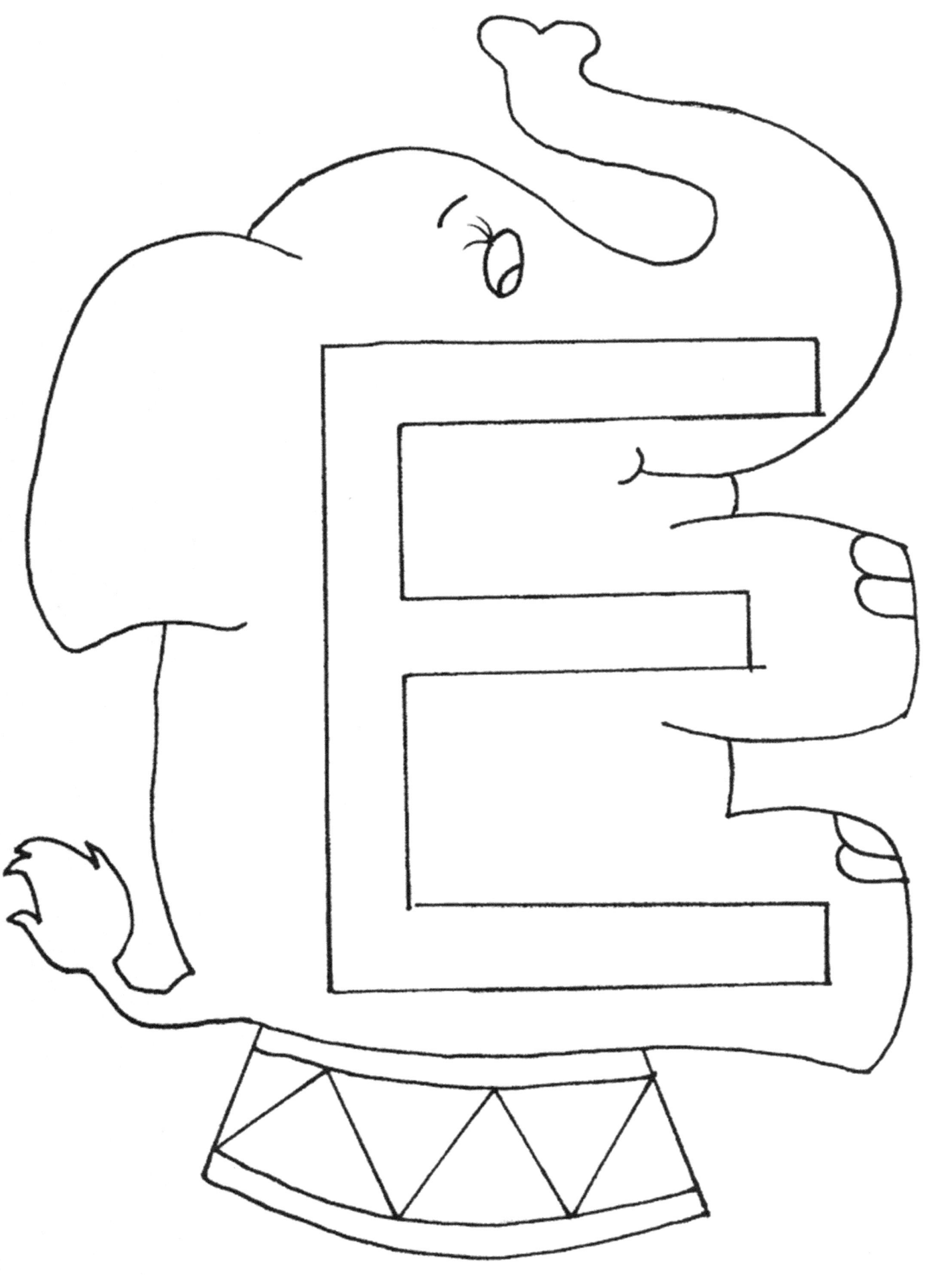

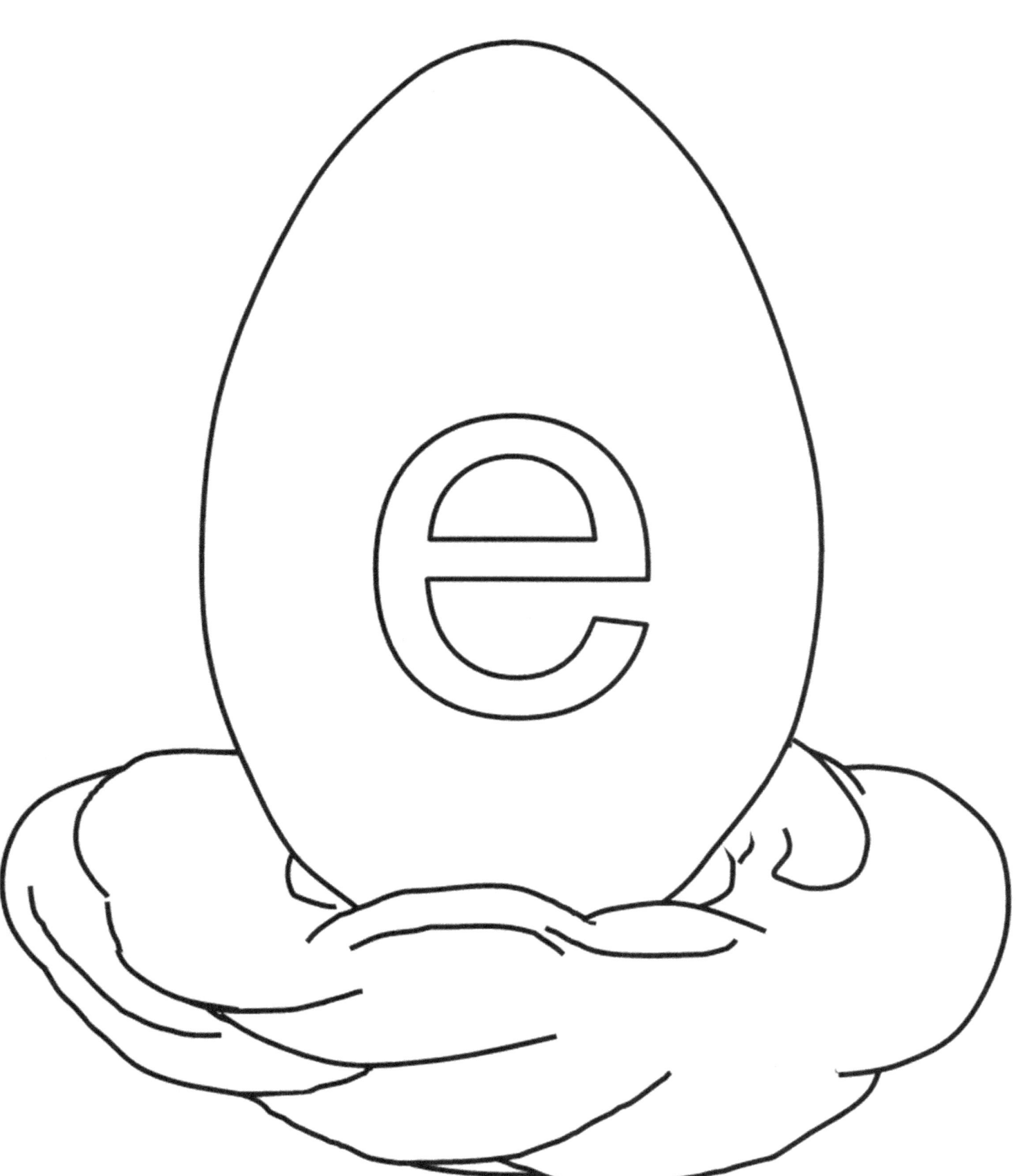

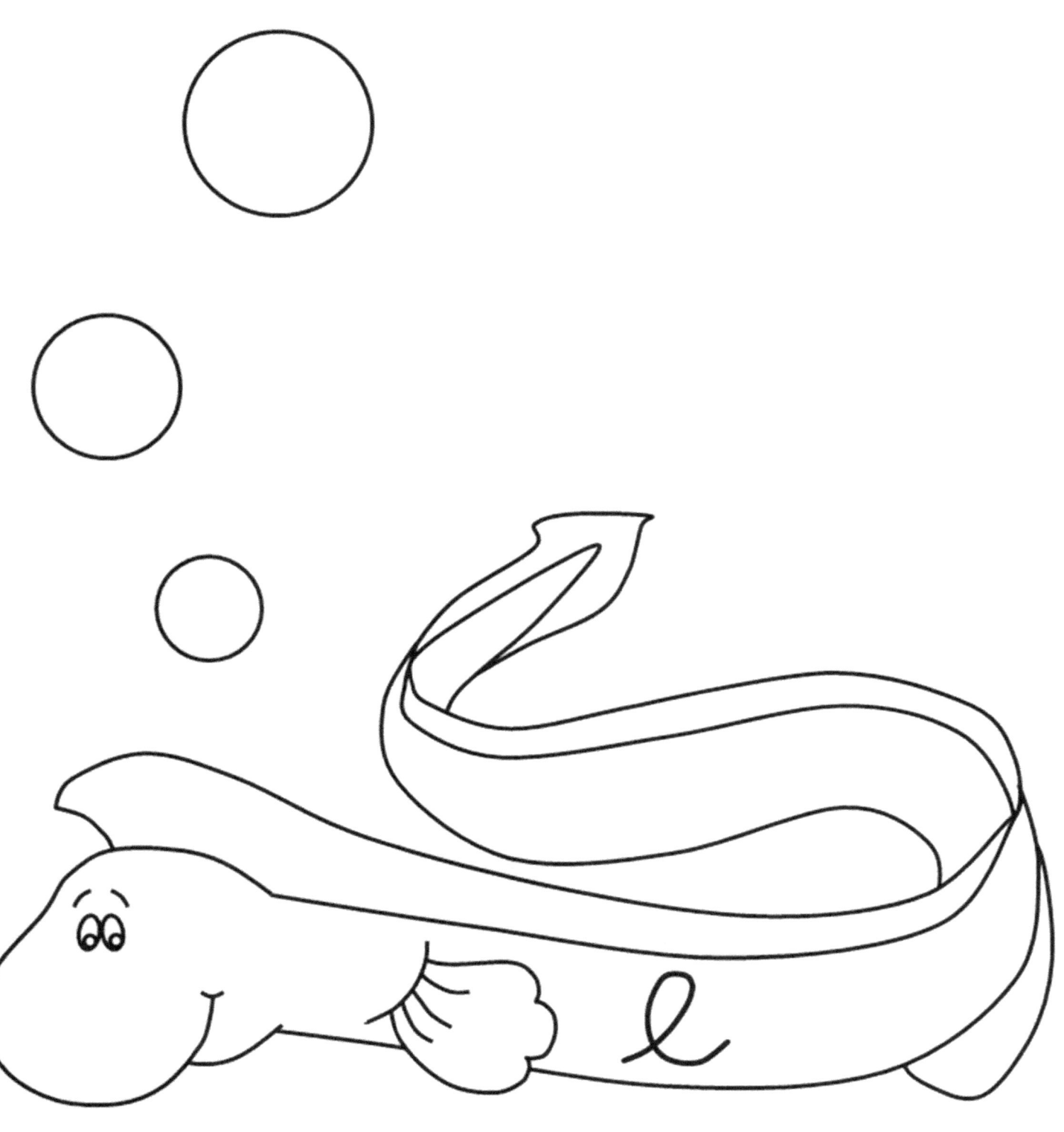

Trace the steps for making the letter e on the following line.

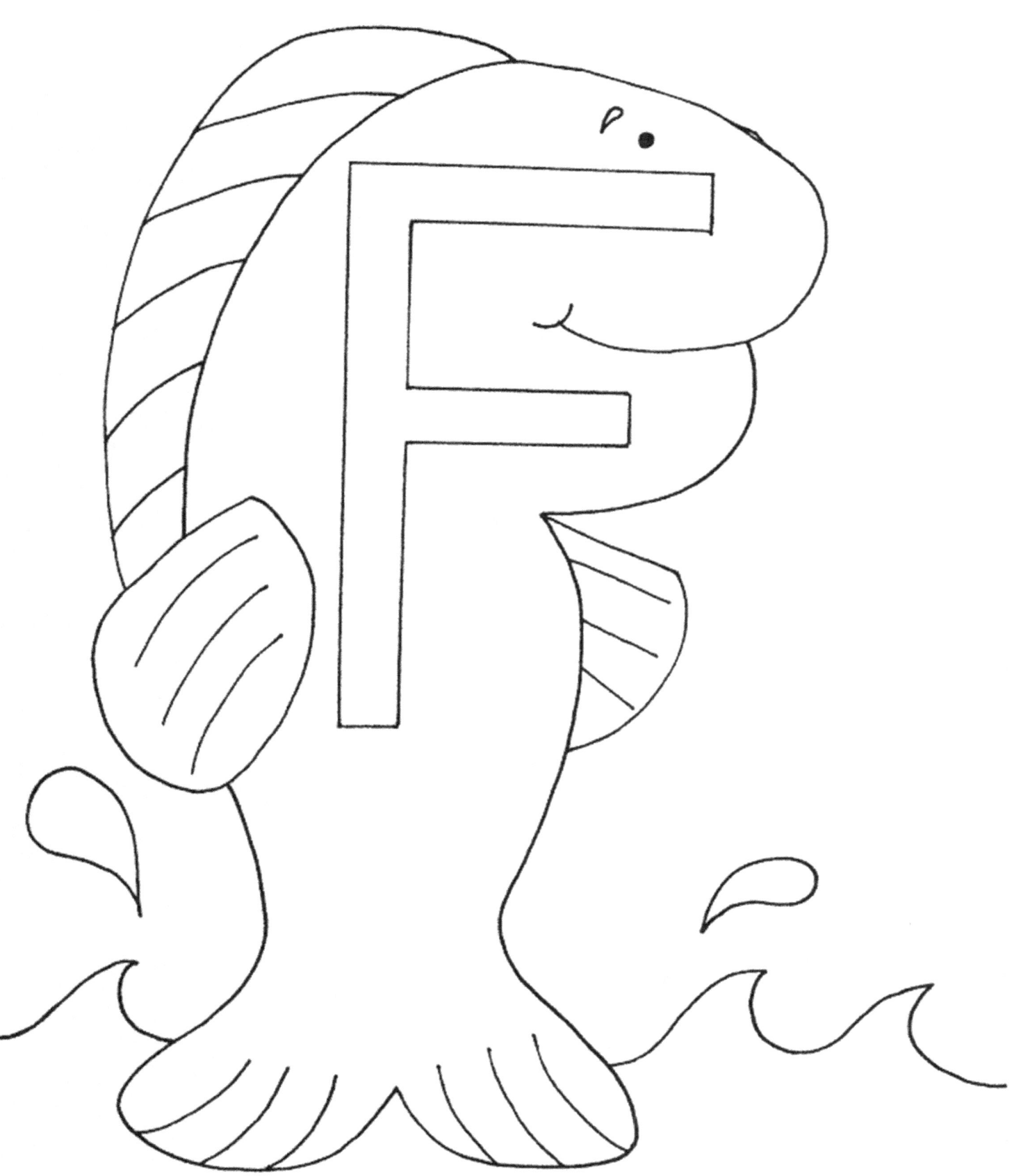

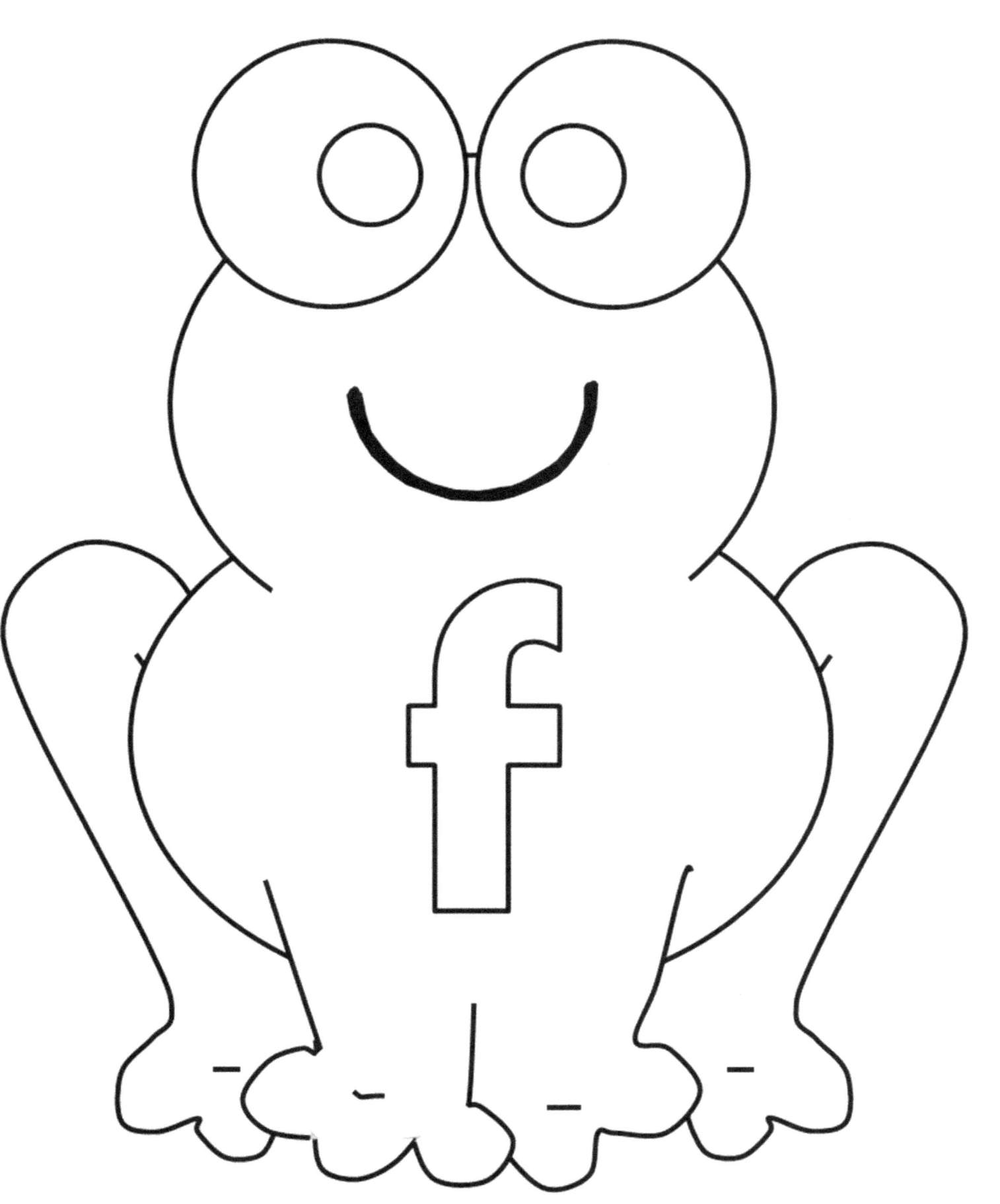

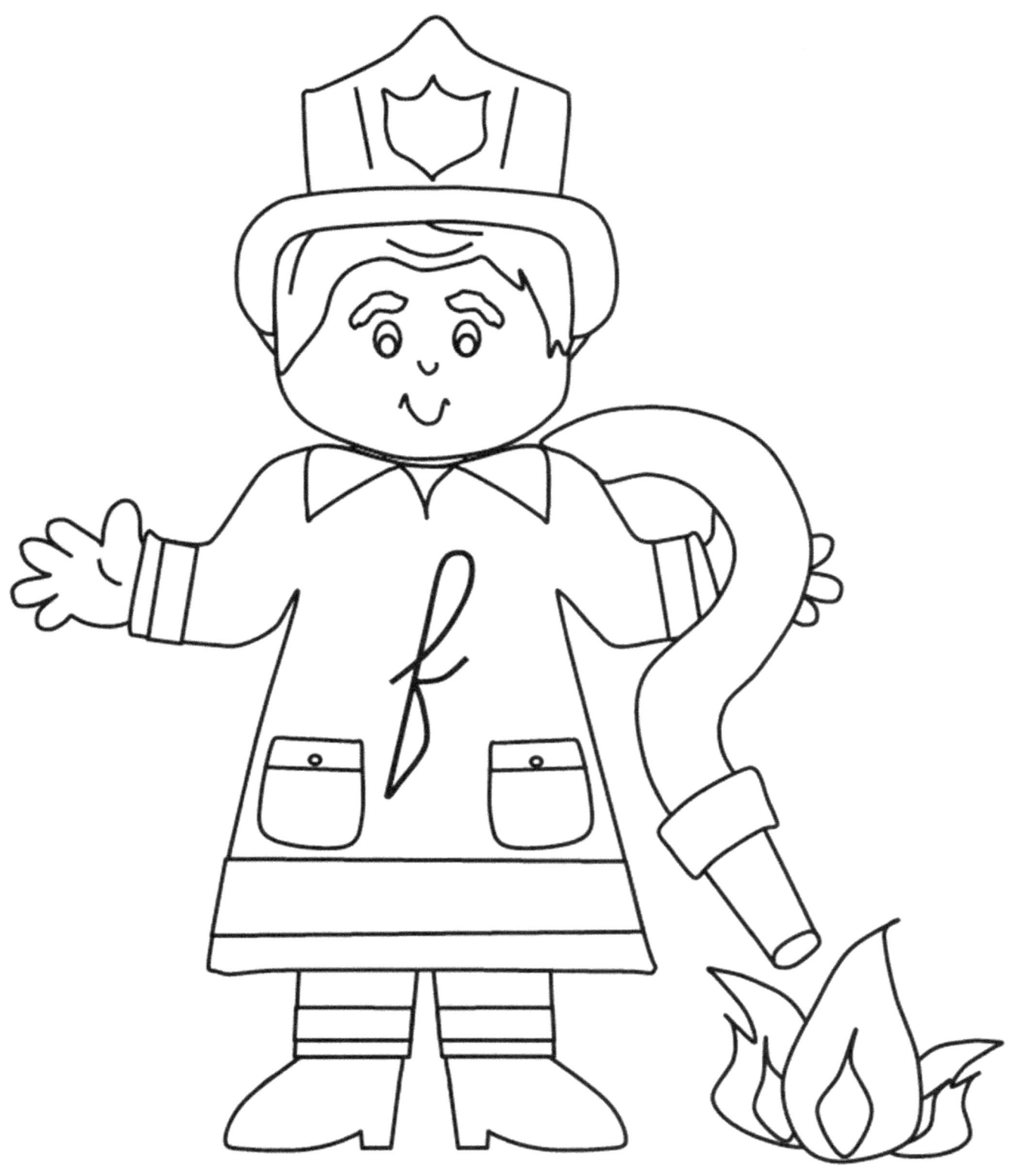

Trace the steps for making the letter f on the following line.

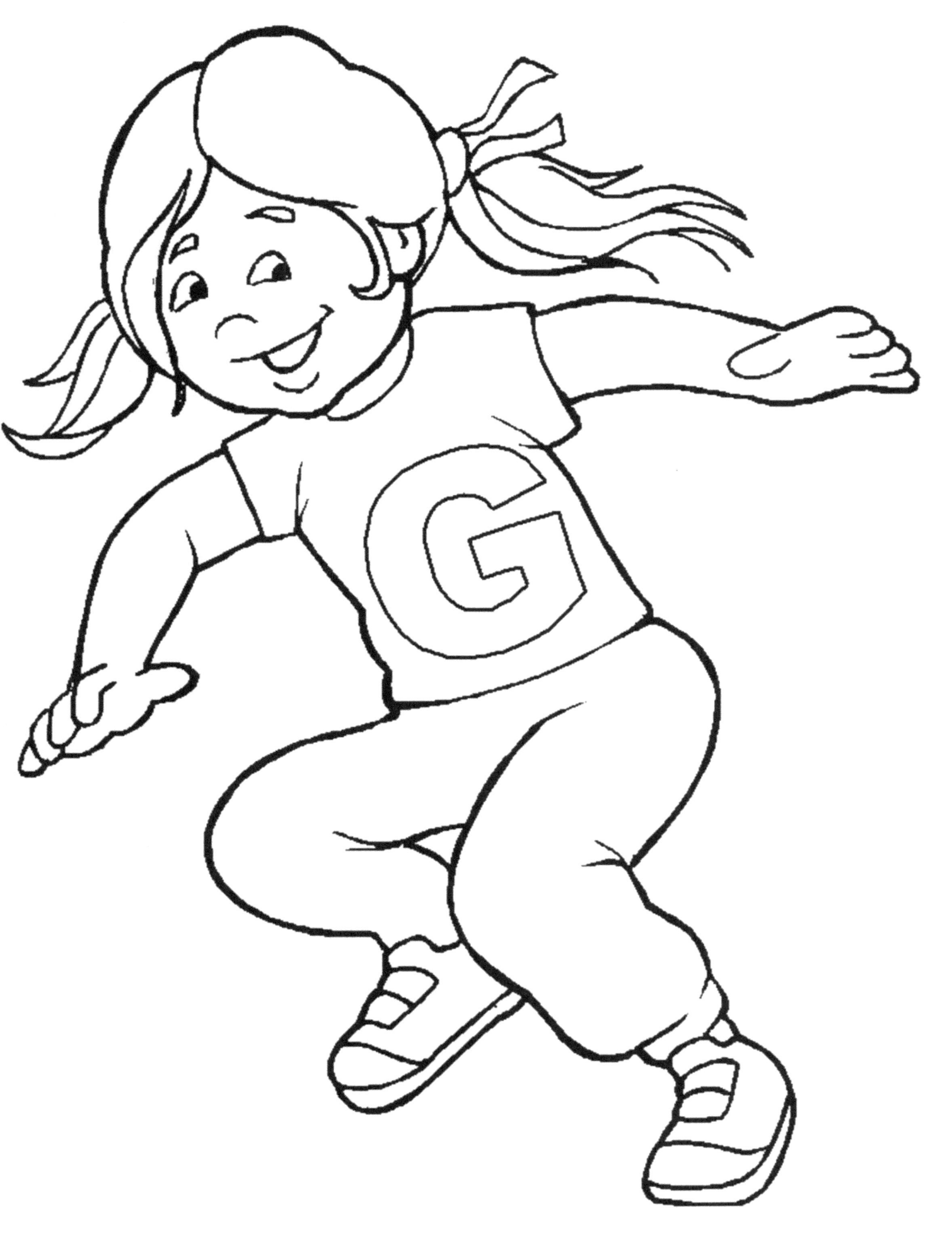

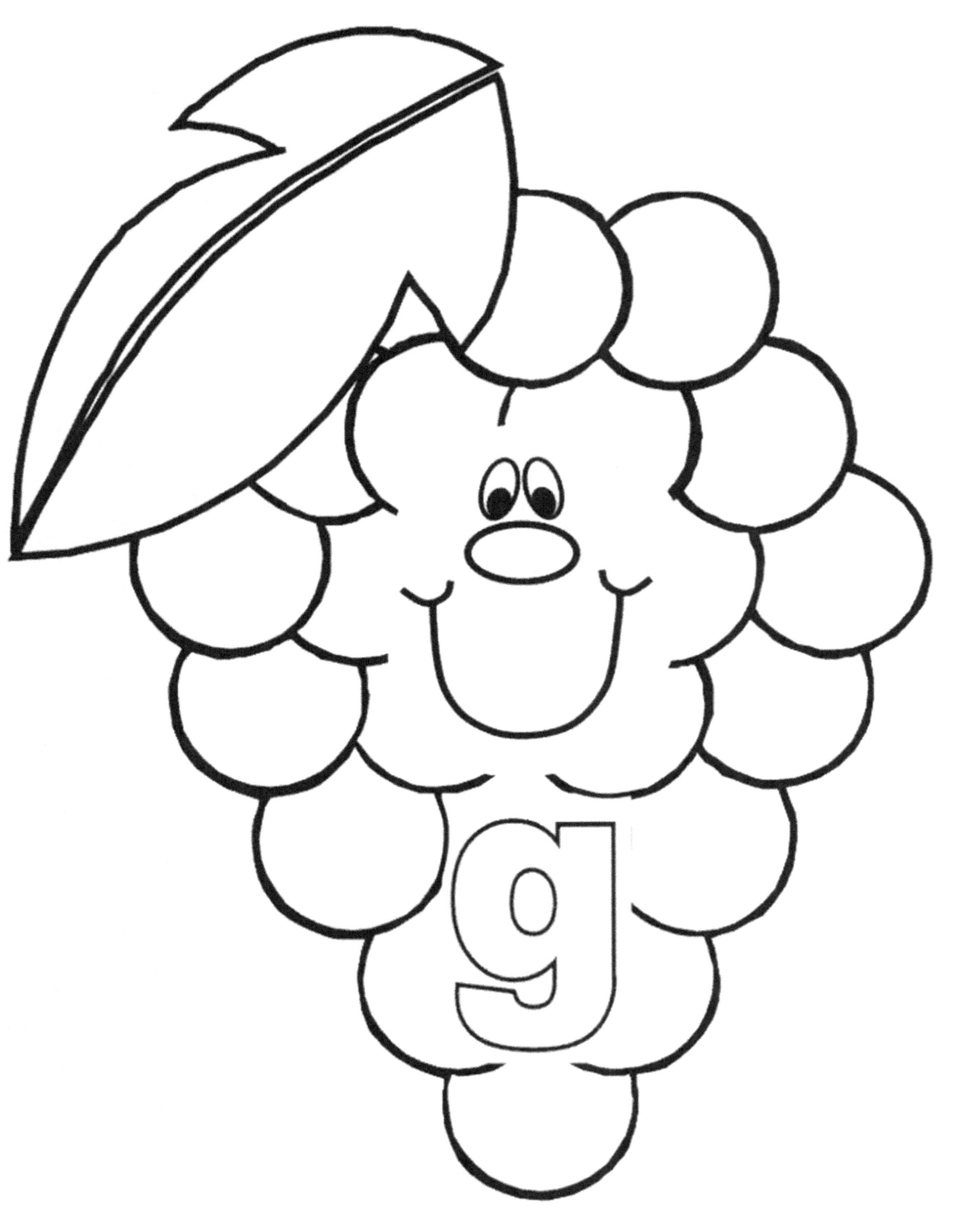

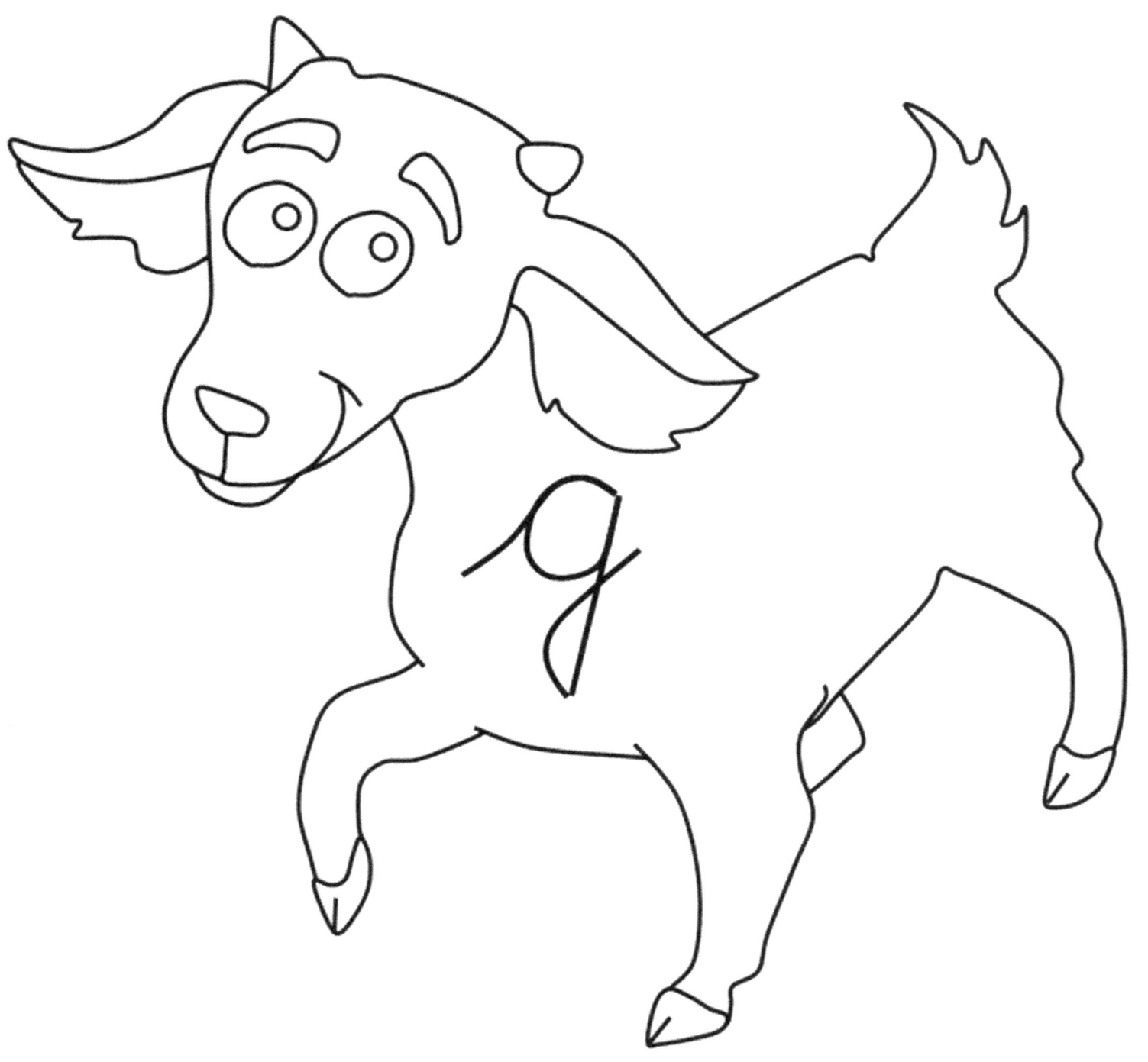

Trace the steps for making the letter g on the following line.

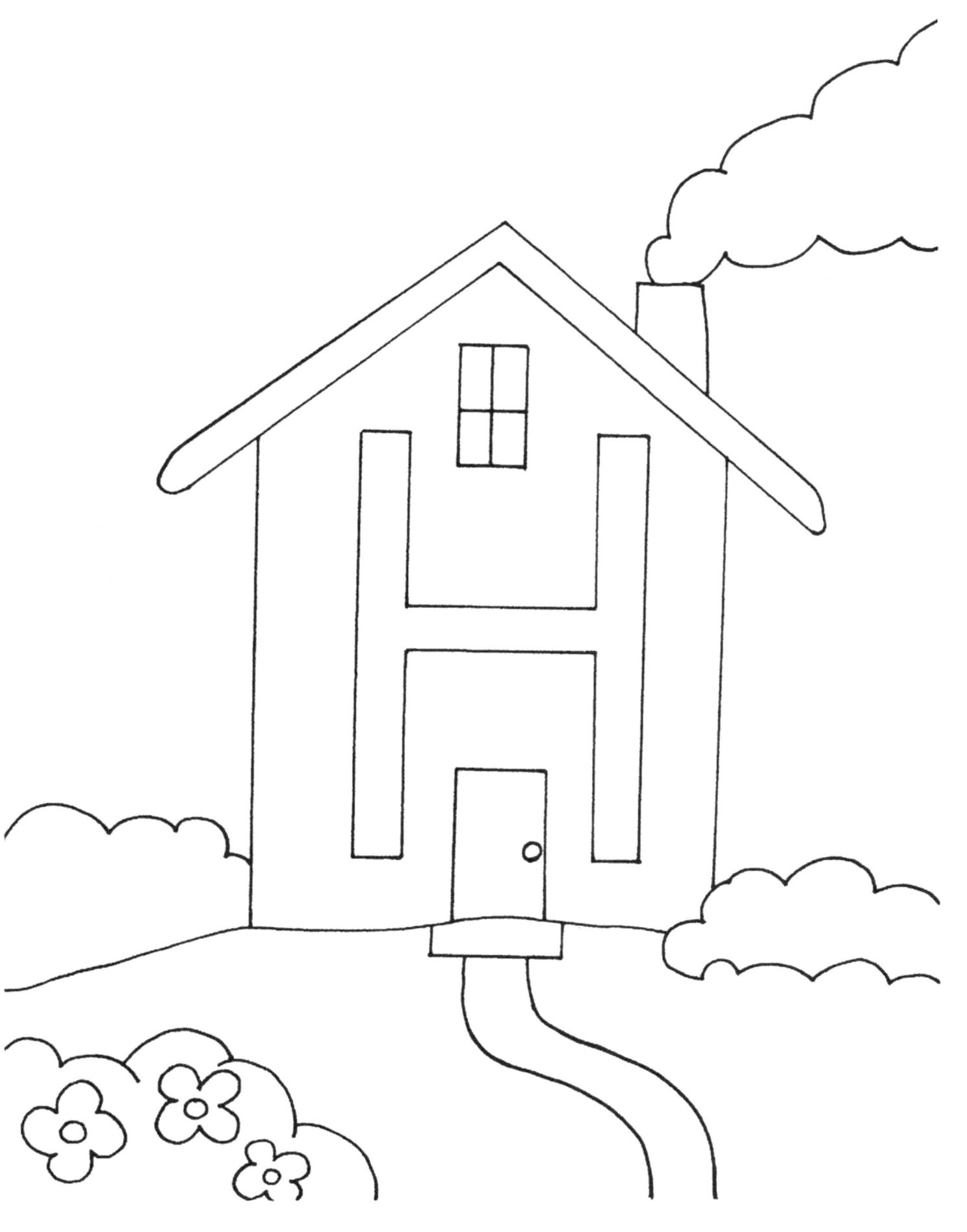

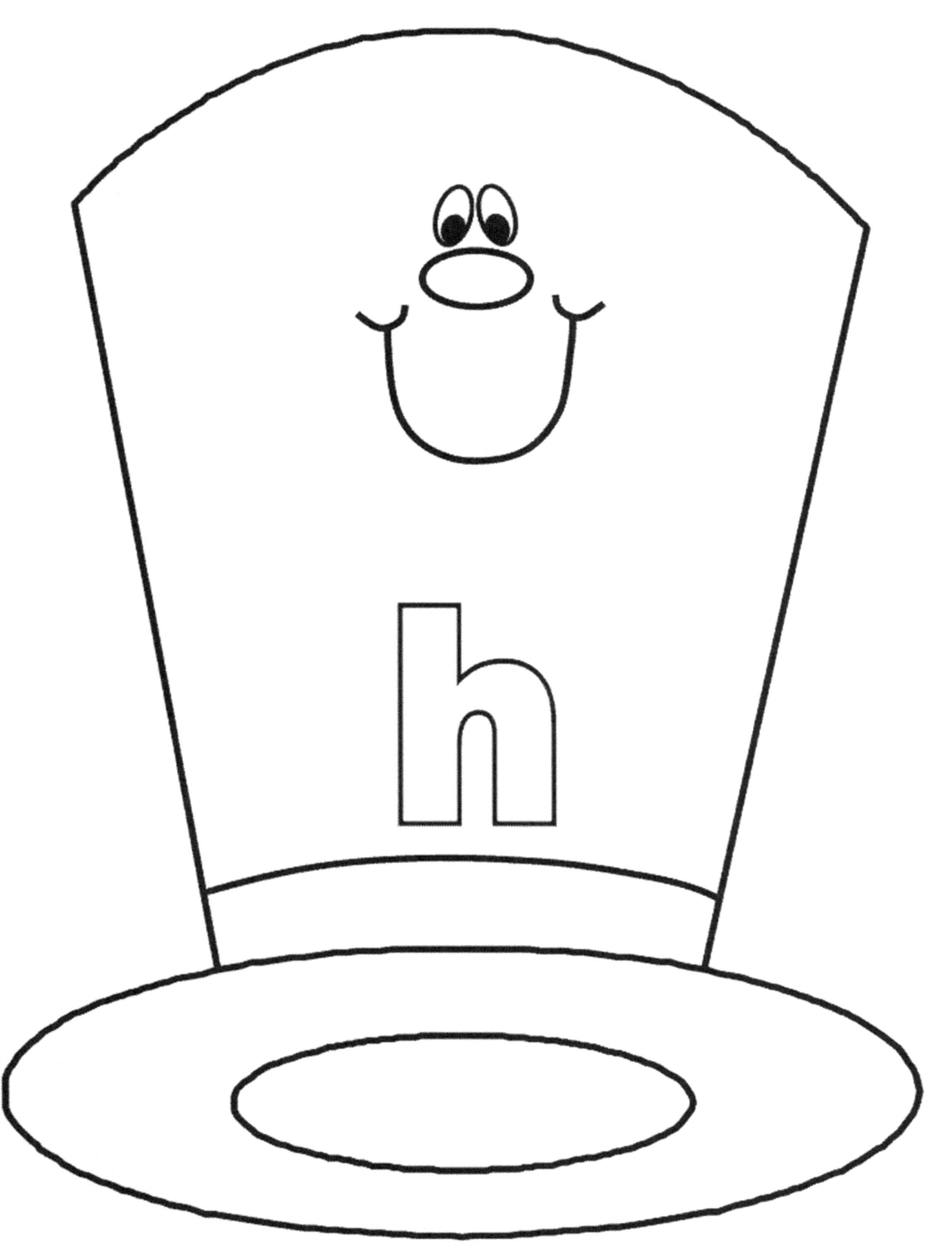

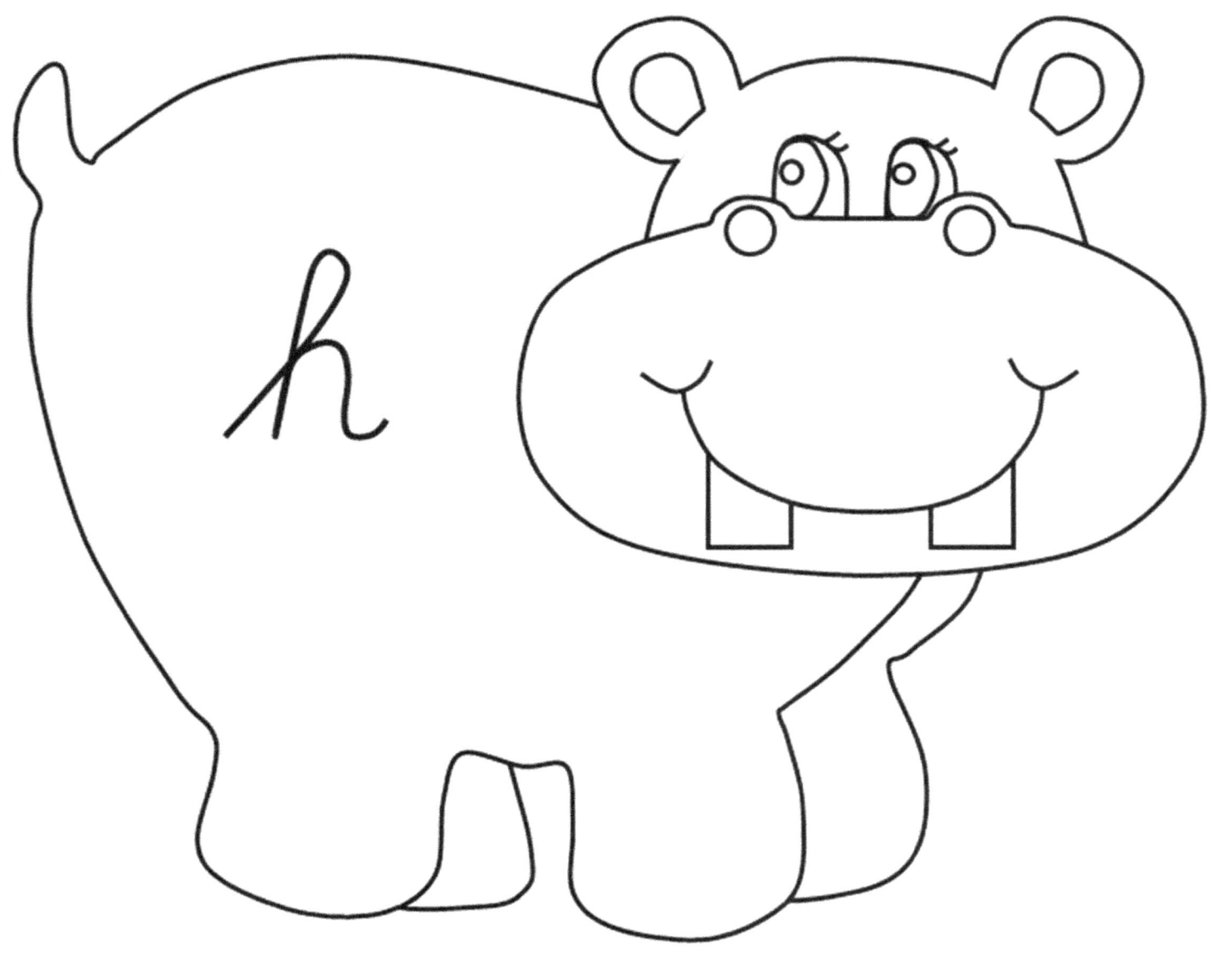

Trace the steps for making the letter h on the following line.

$h$ $h$ $h$ $h$ $h$ $hh$

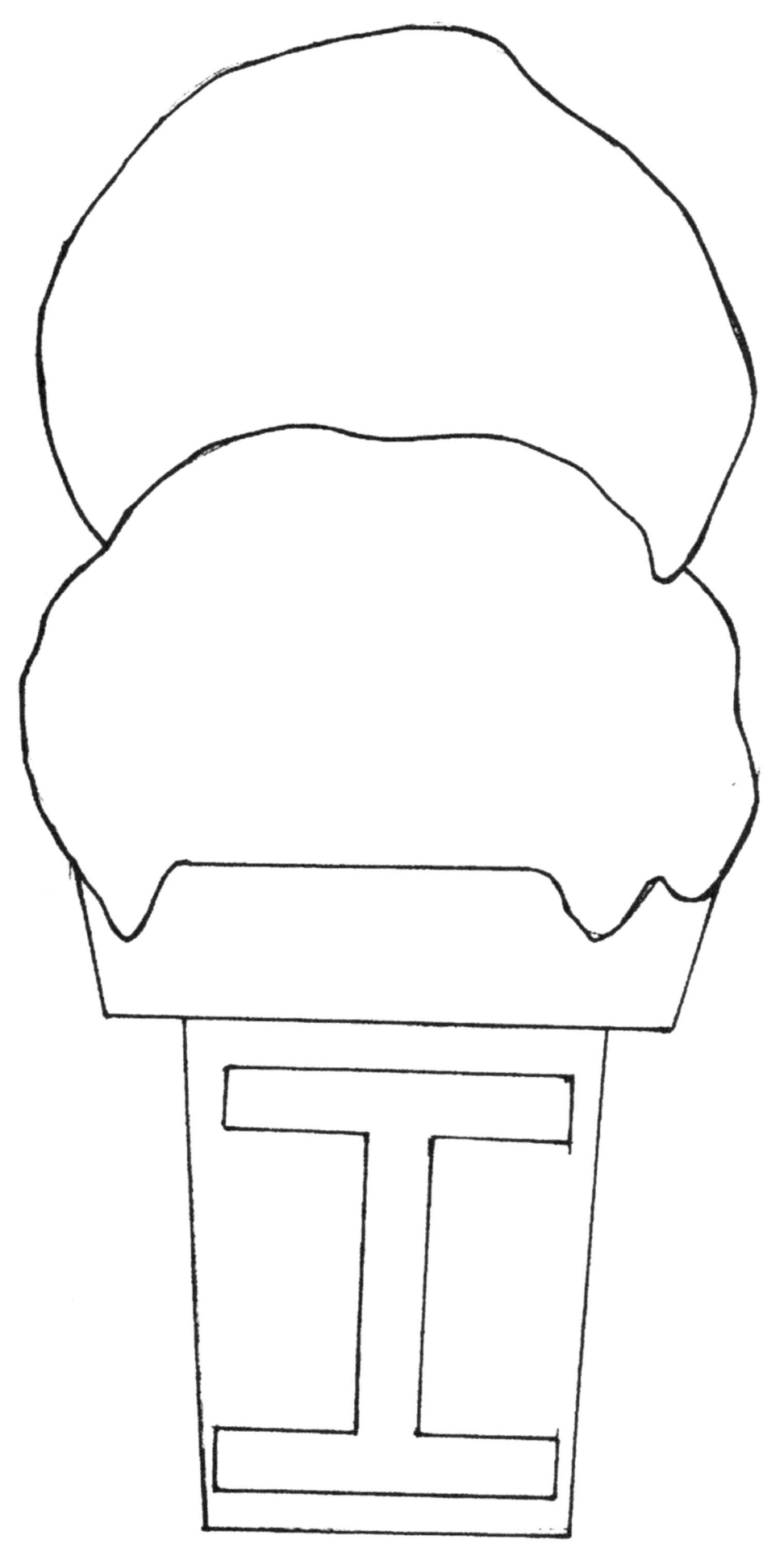

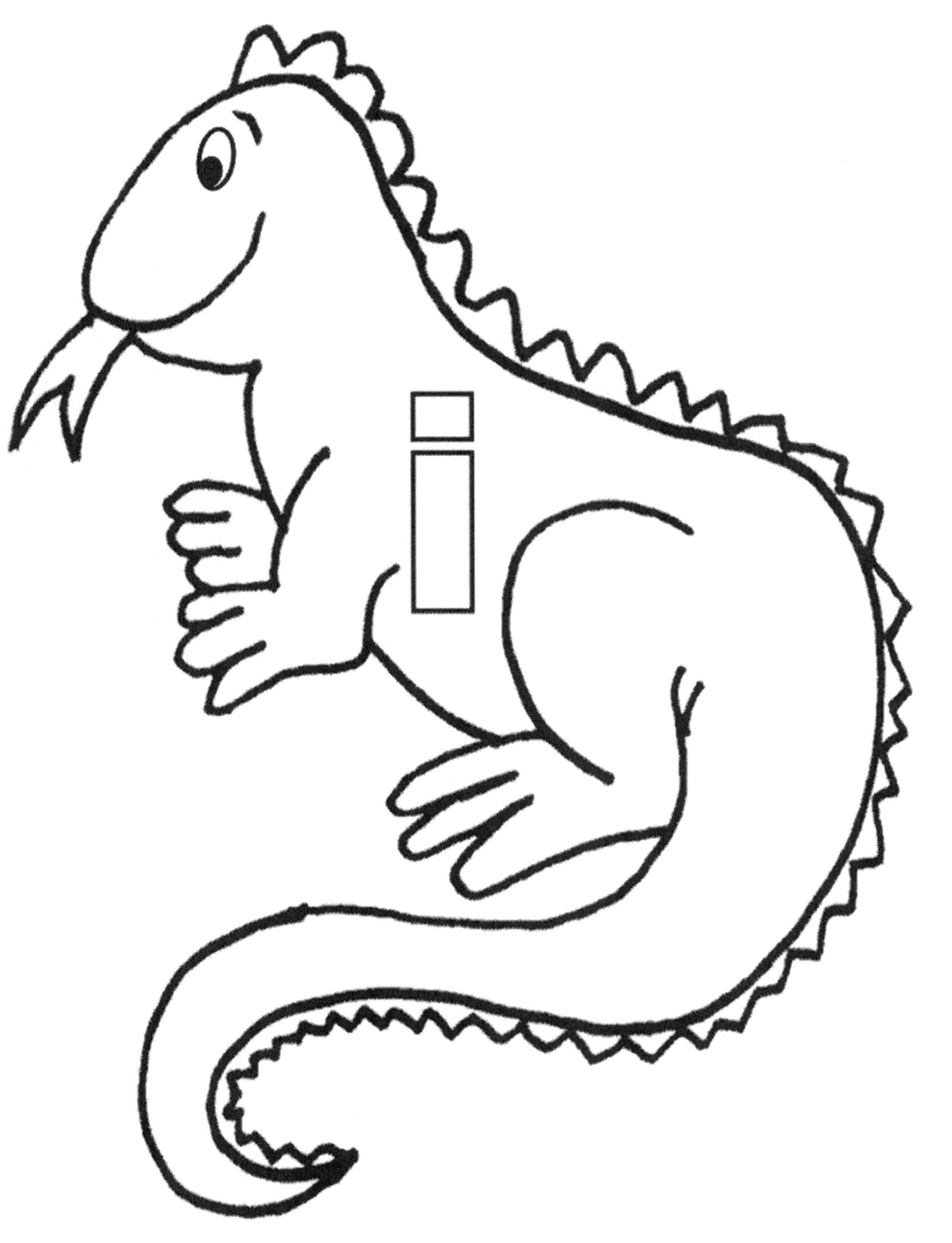

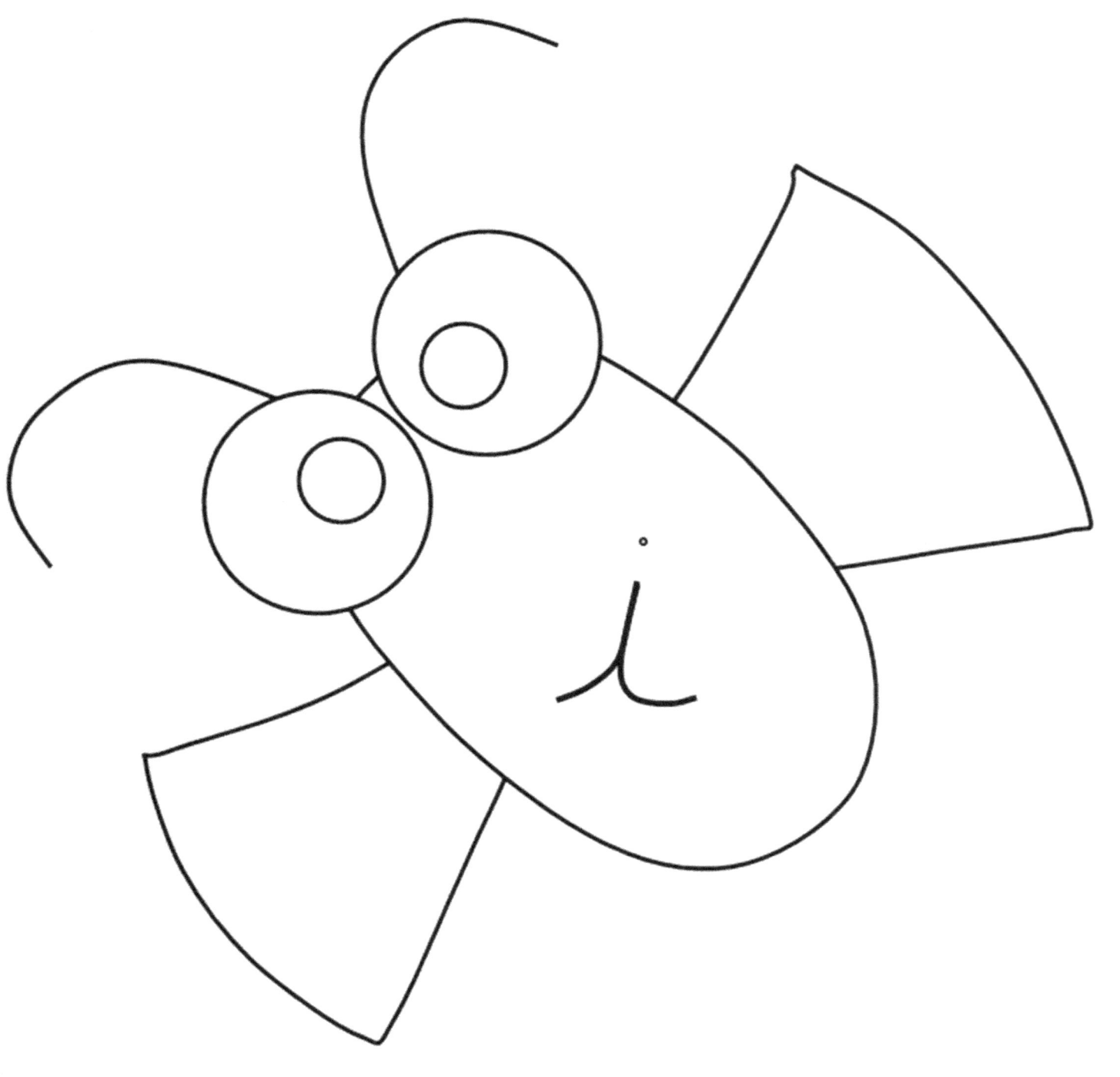

Trace the steps for making the letter i on the following line.

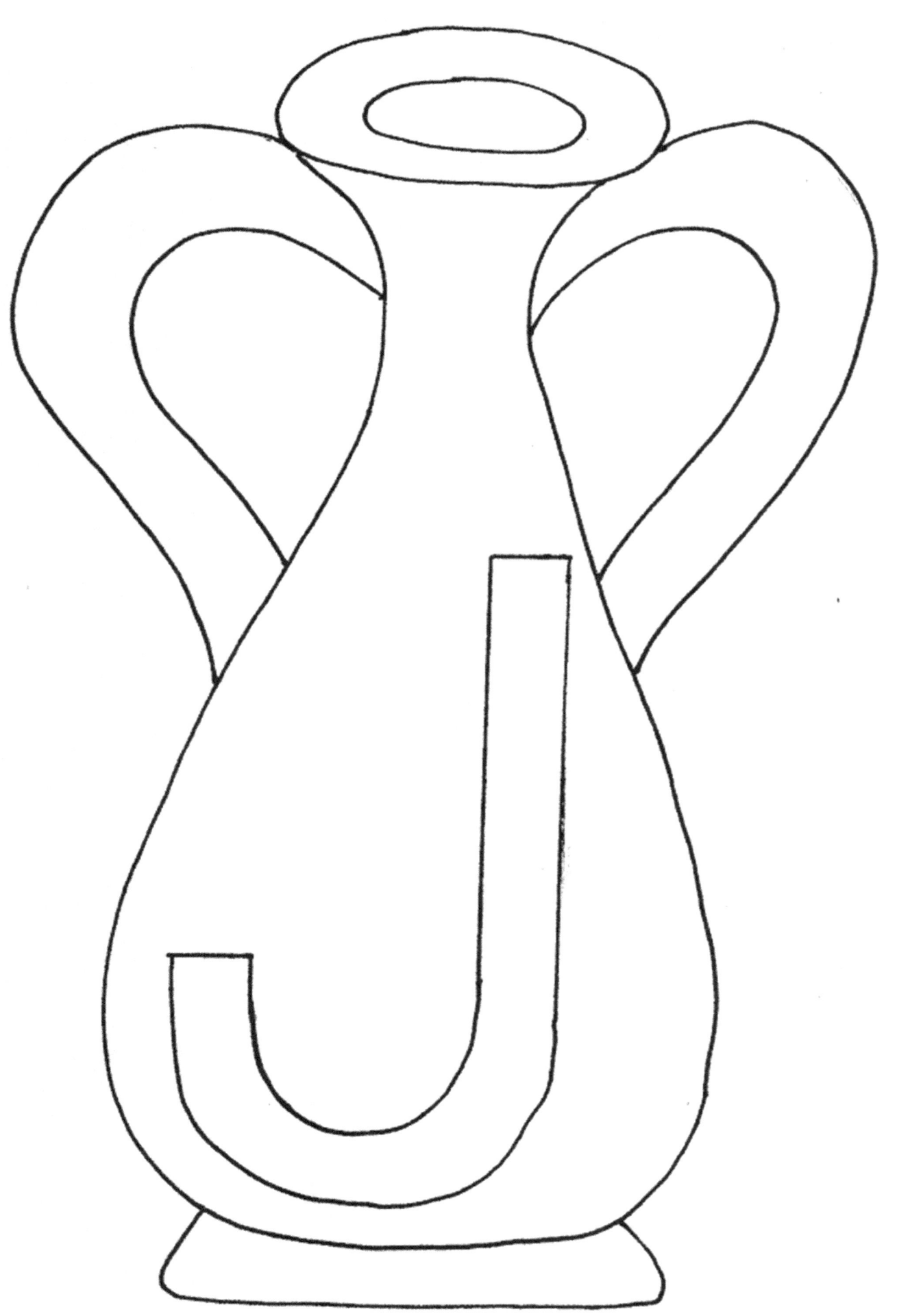

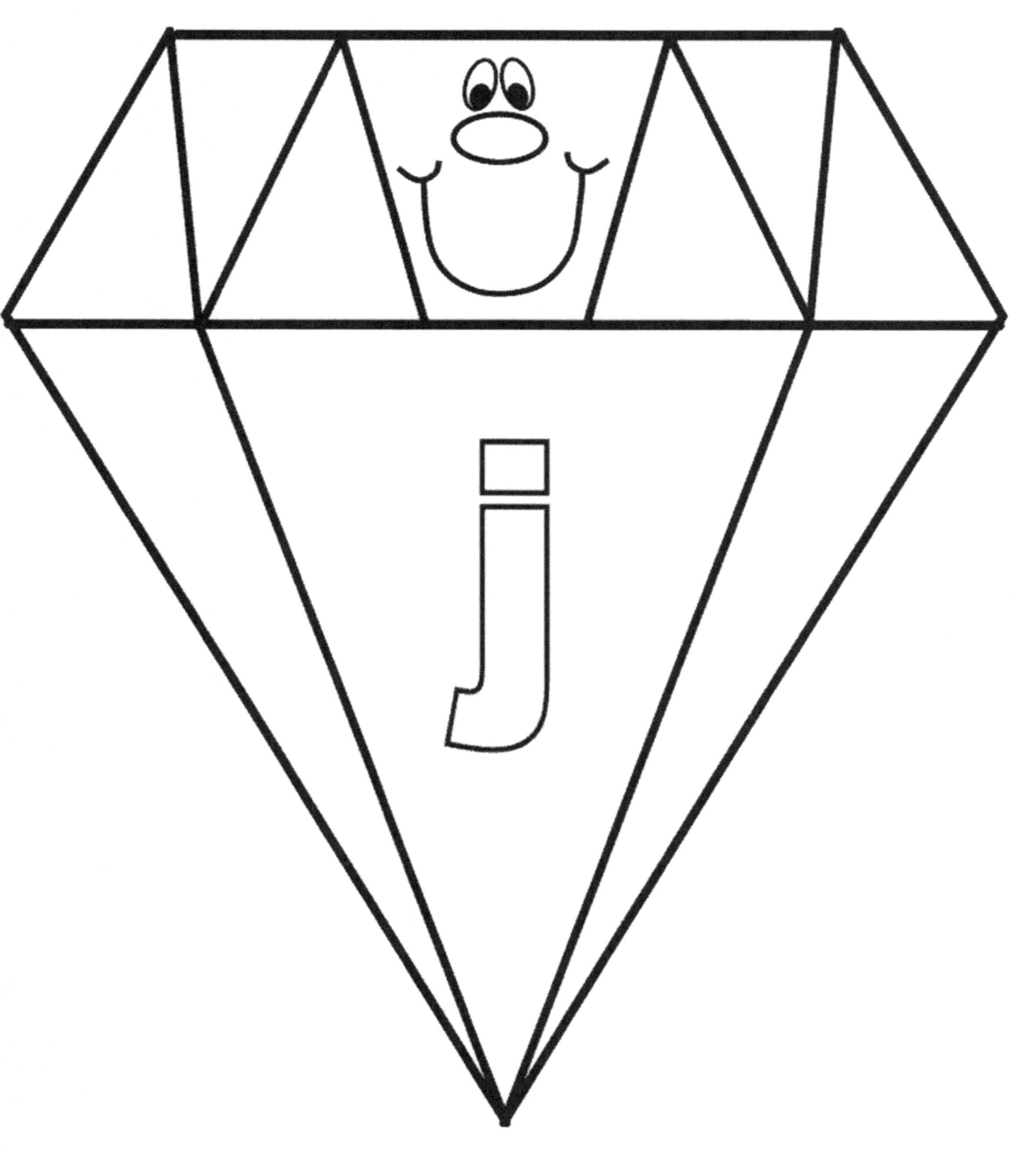

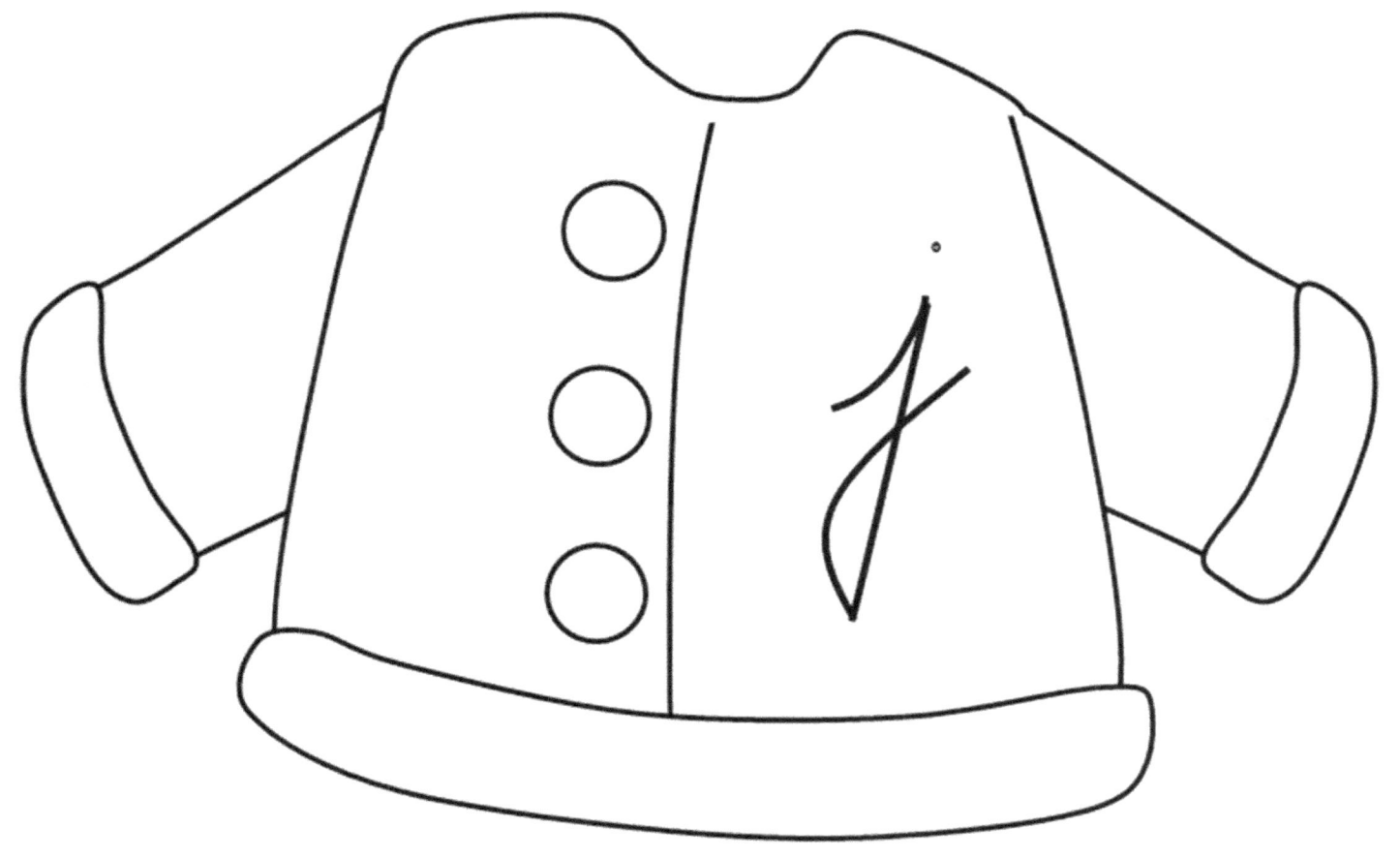

Trace the steps for making the letter j on the following line.

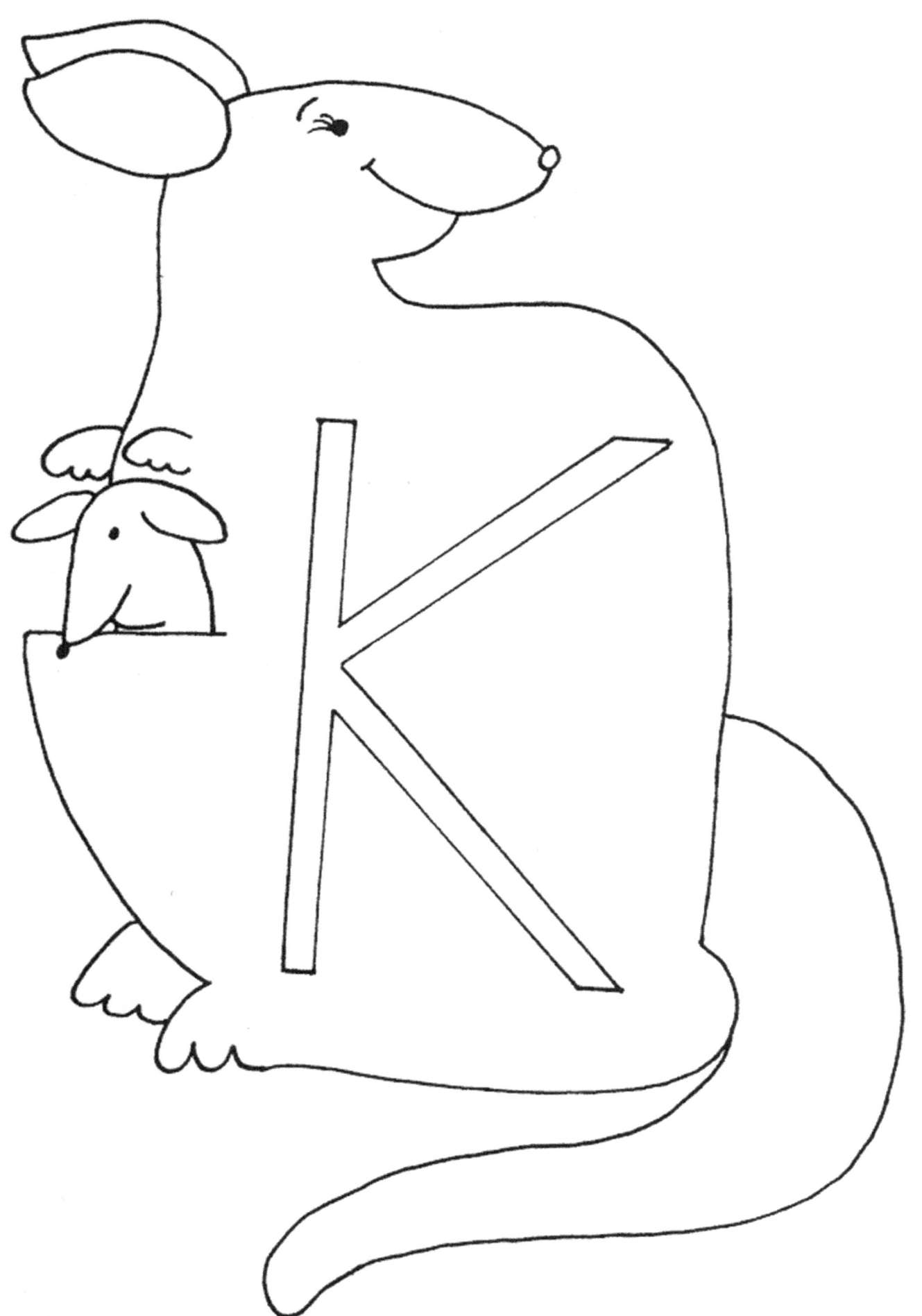

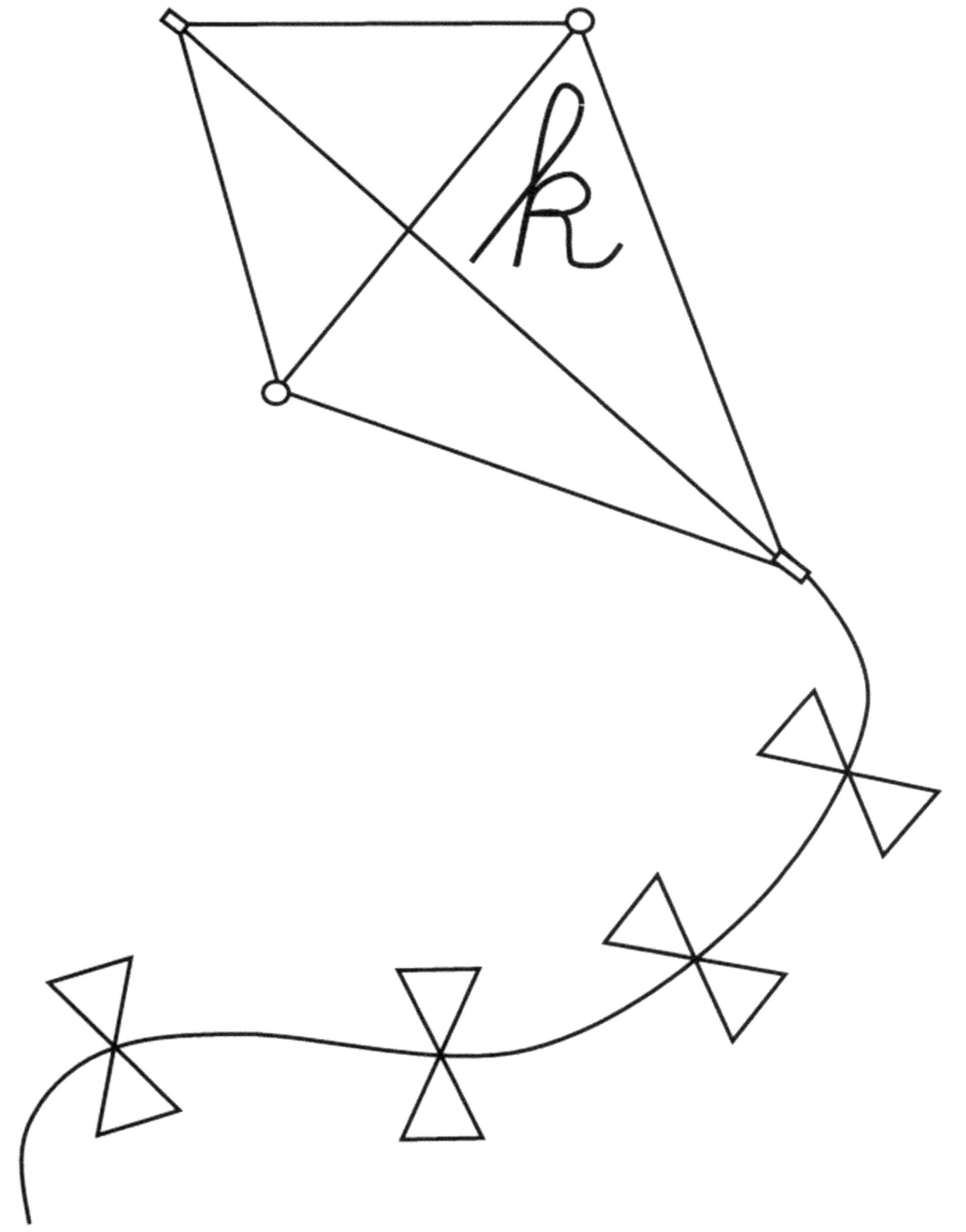

Trace the steps for making the letter k on the following line.

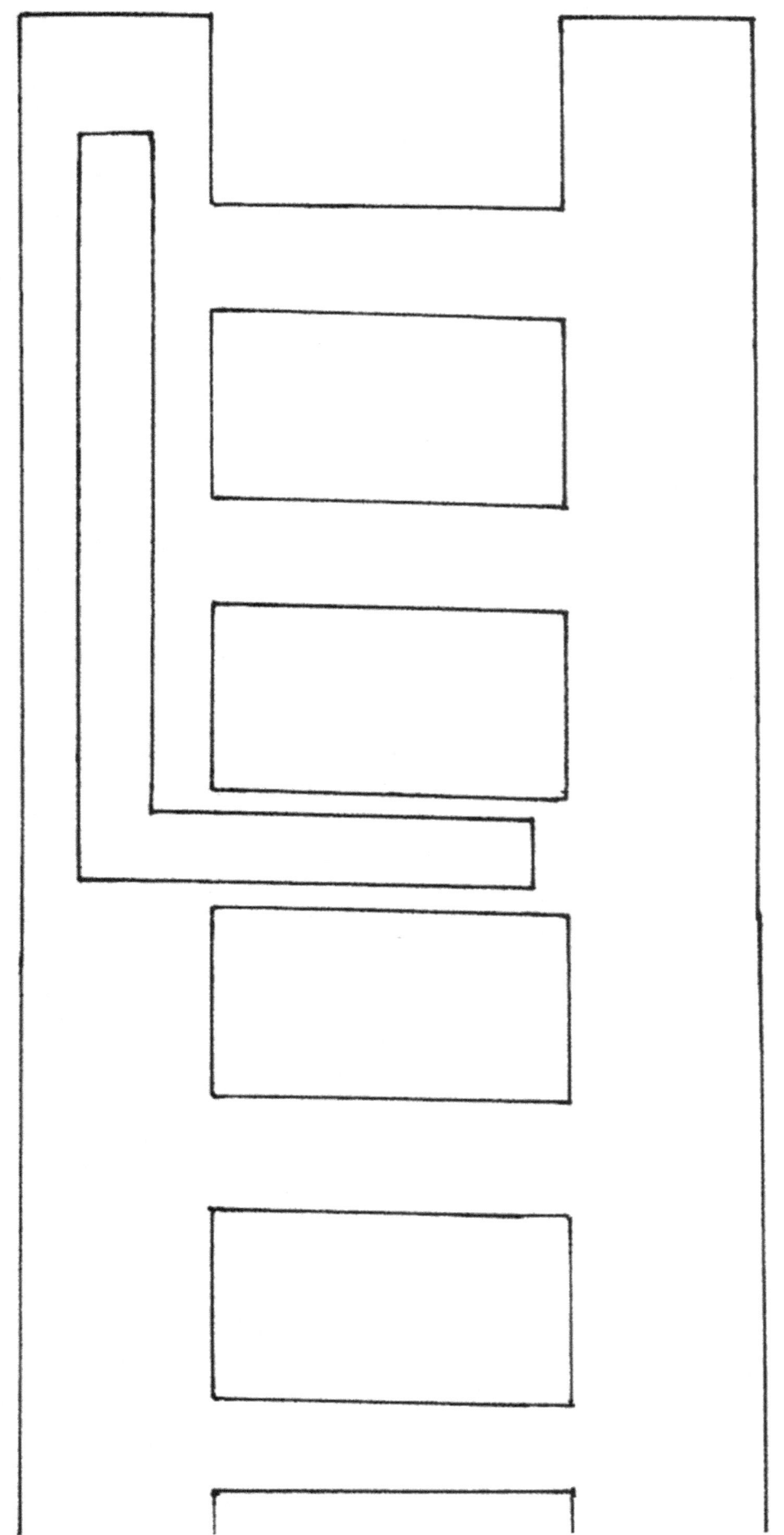

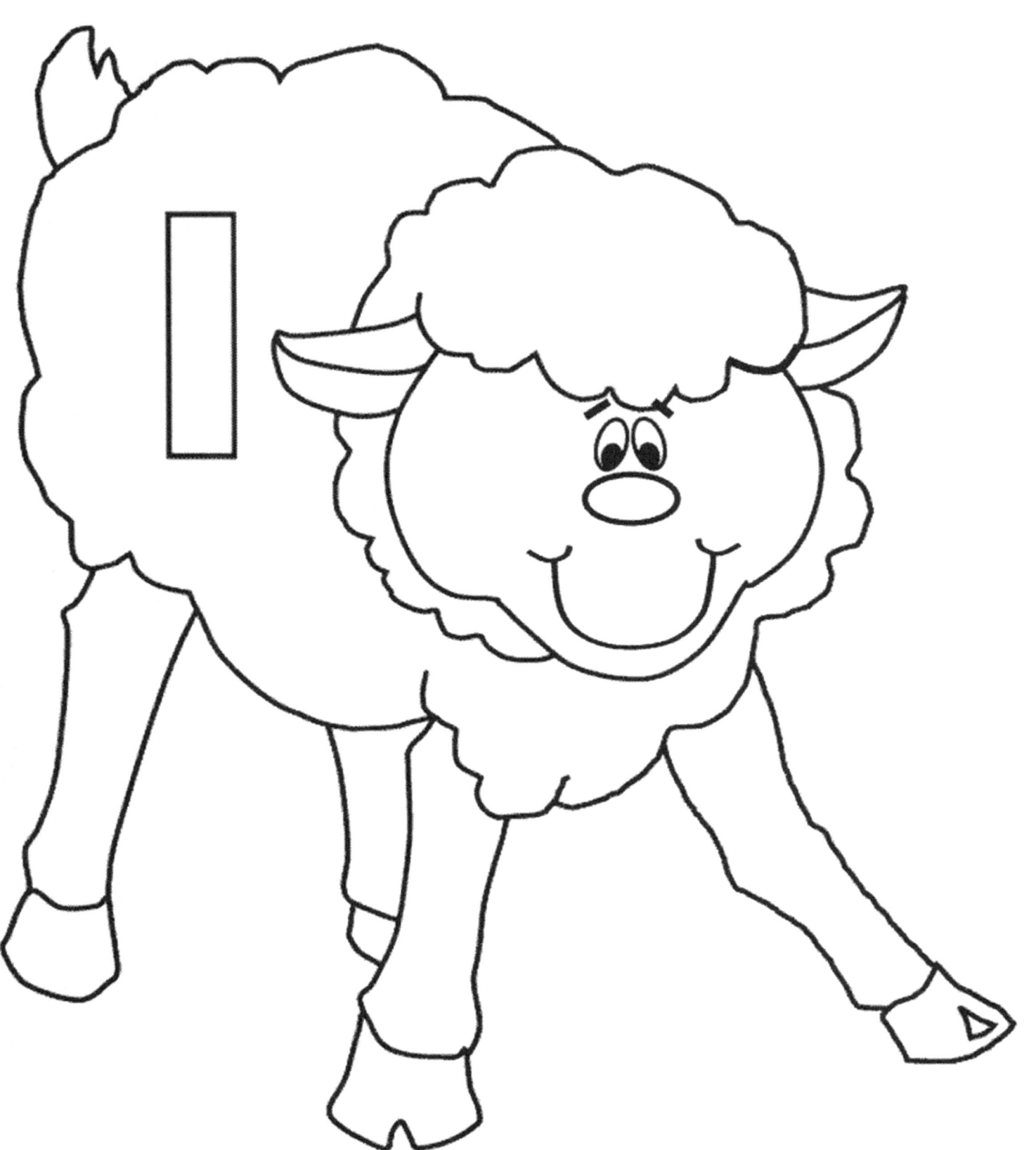

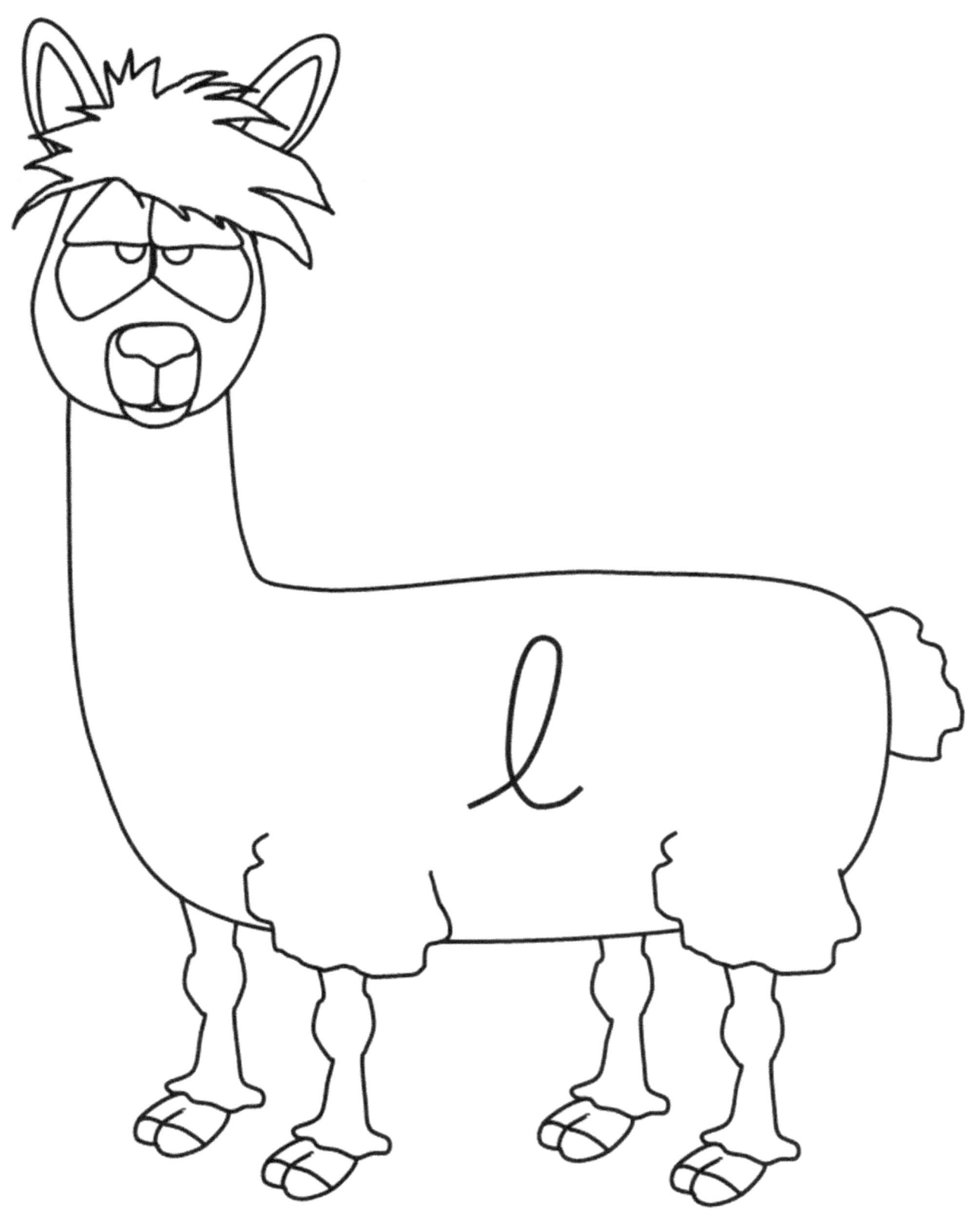

Trace the steps for making the letter l on the following line.

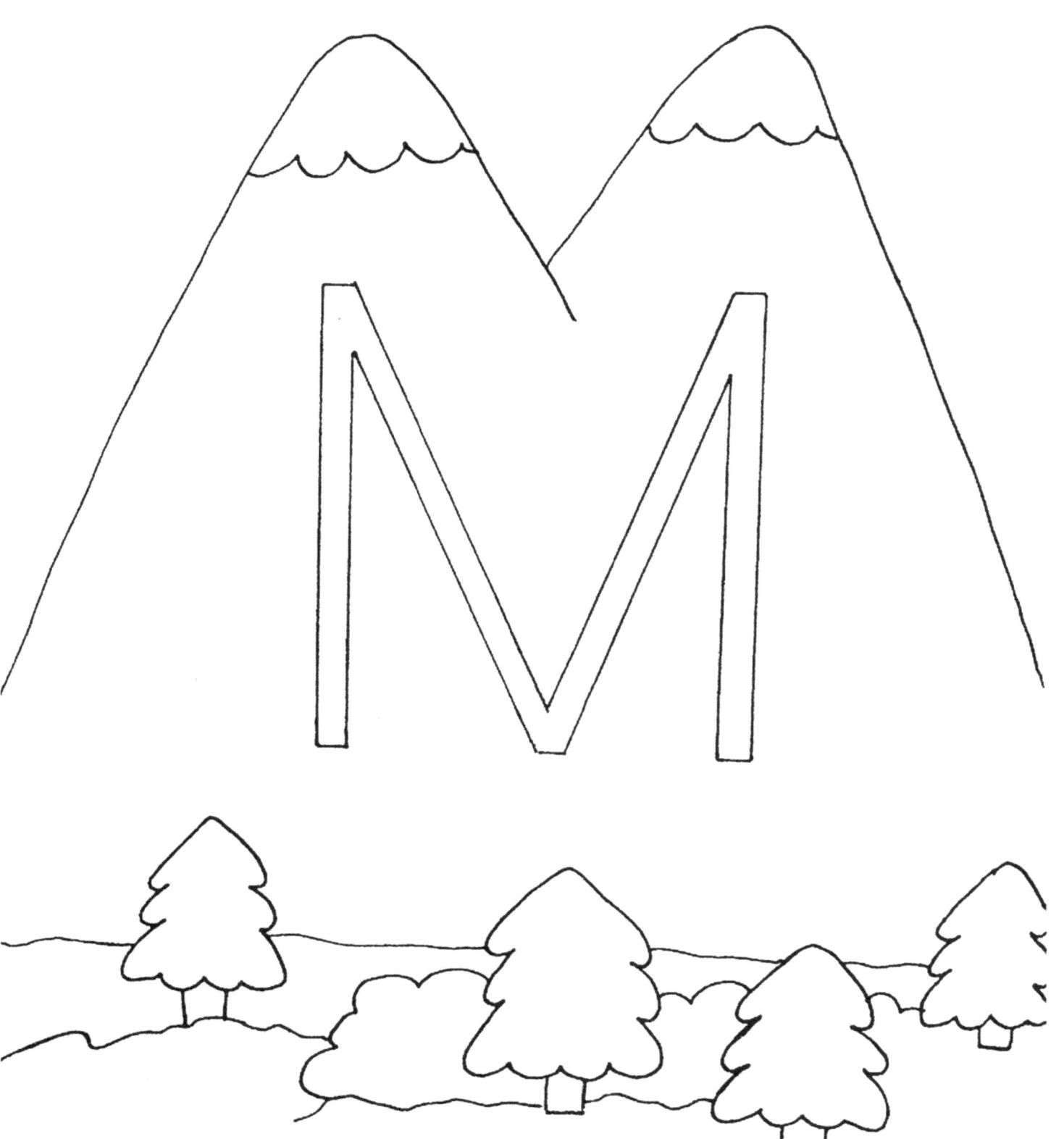

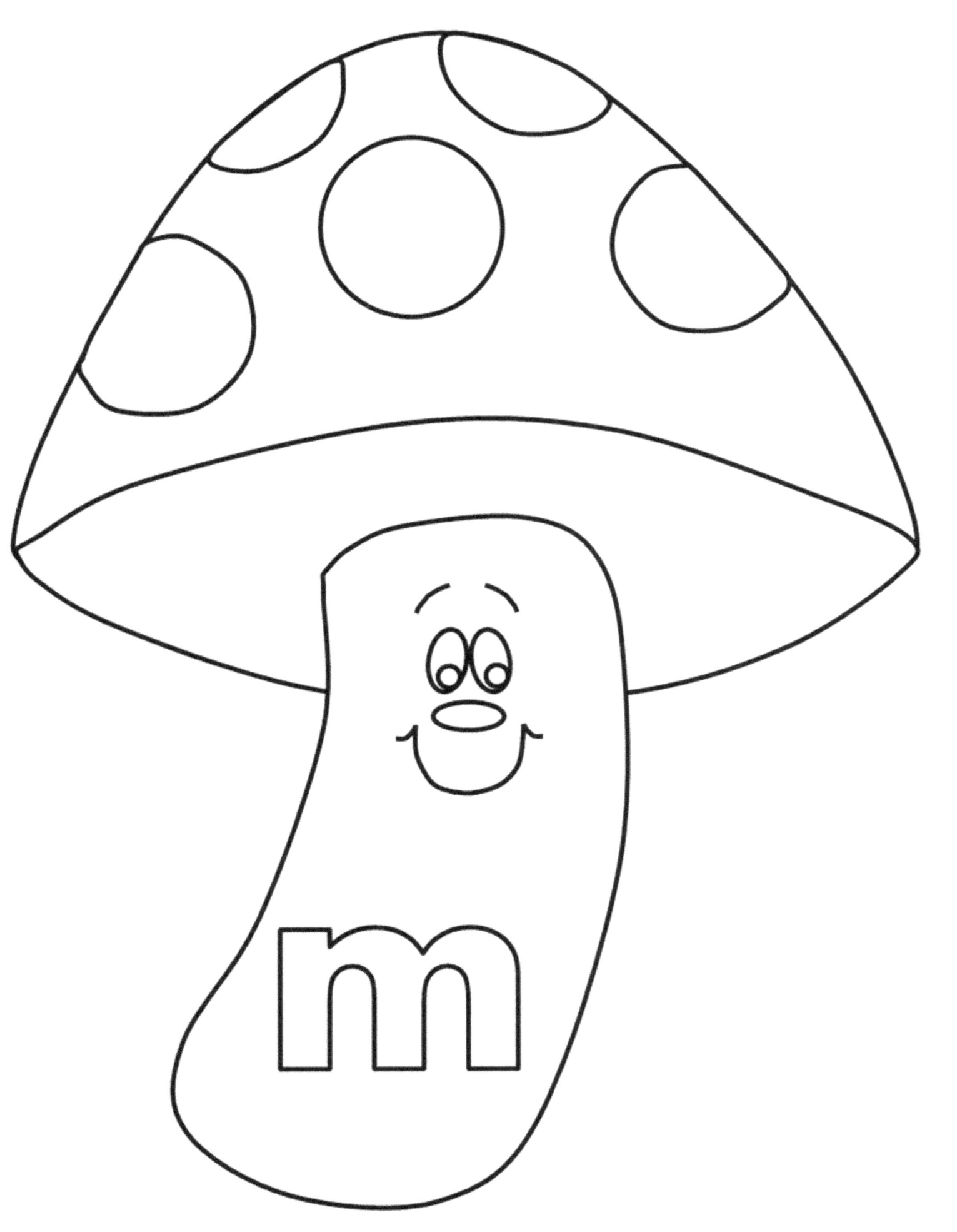

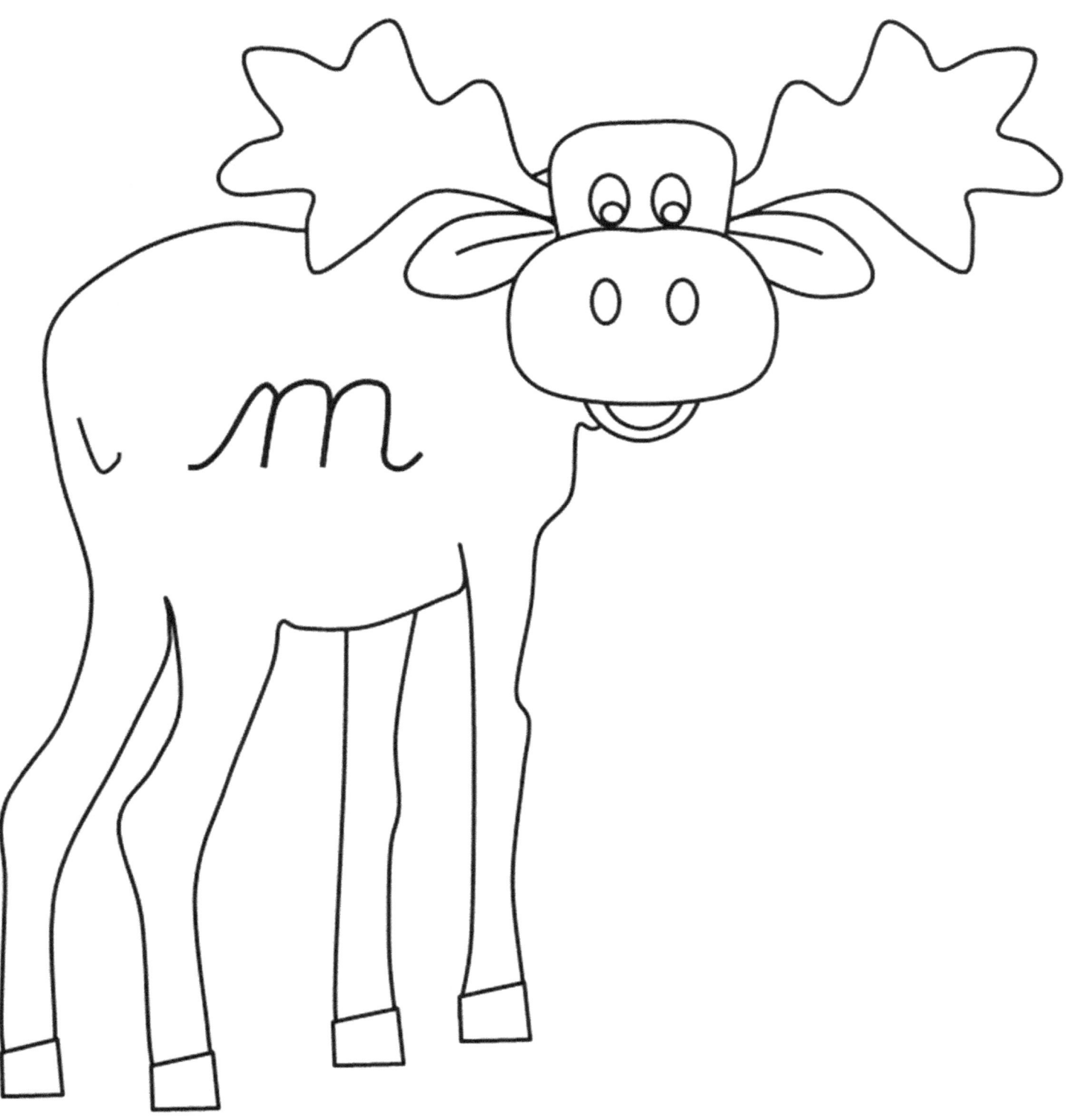

Trace the steps for making the letter m on the following line.

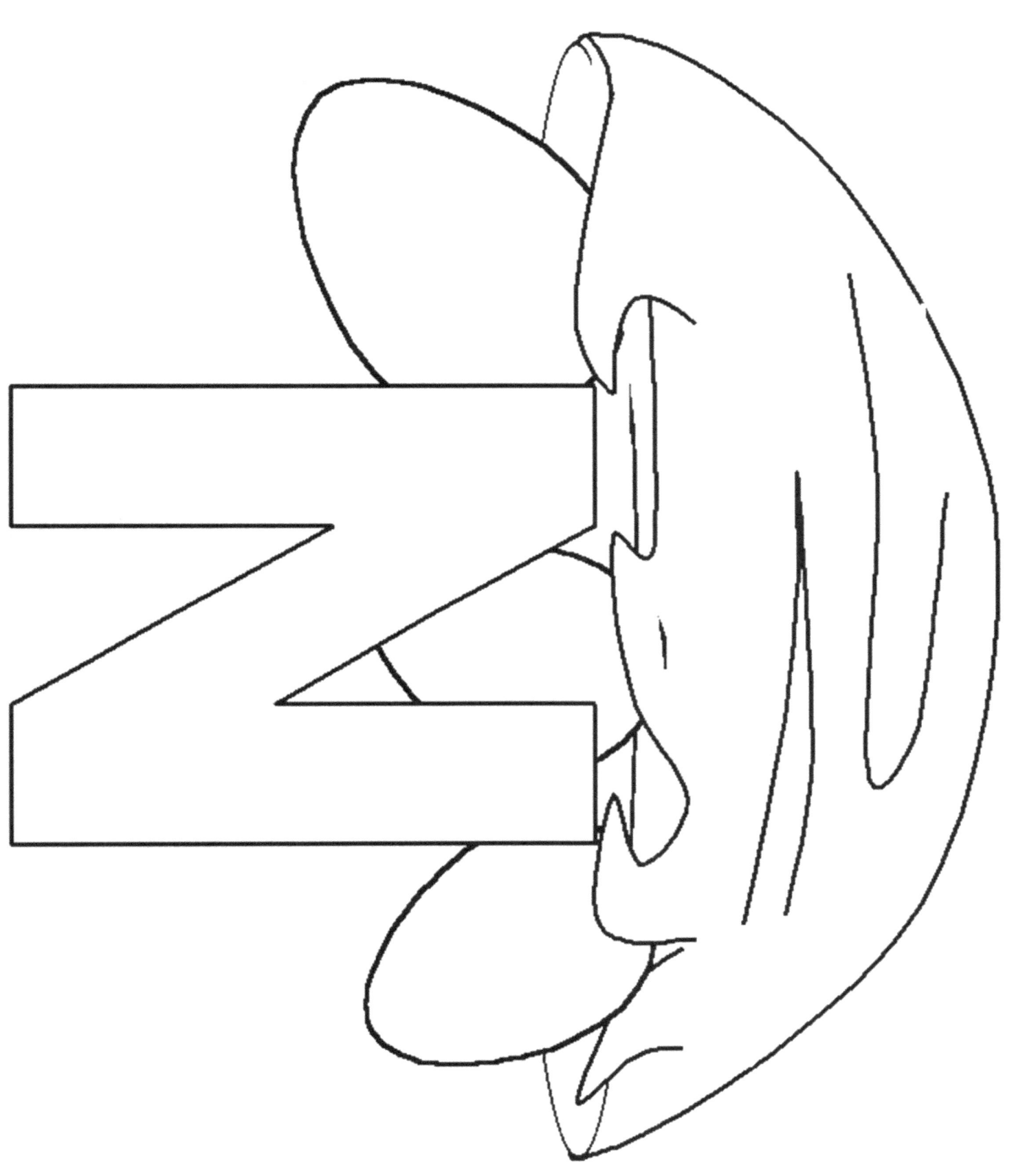

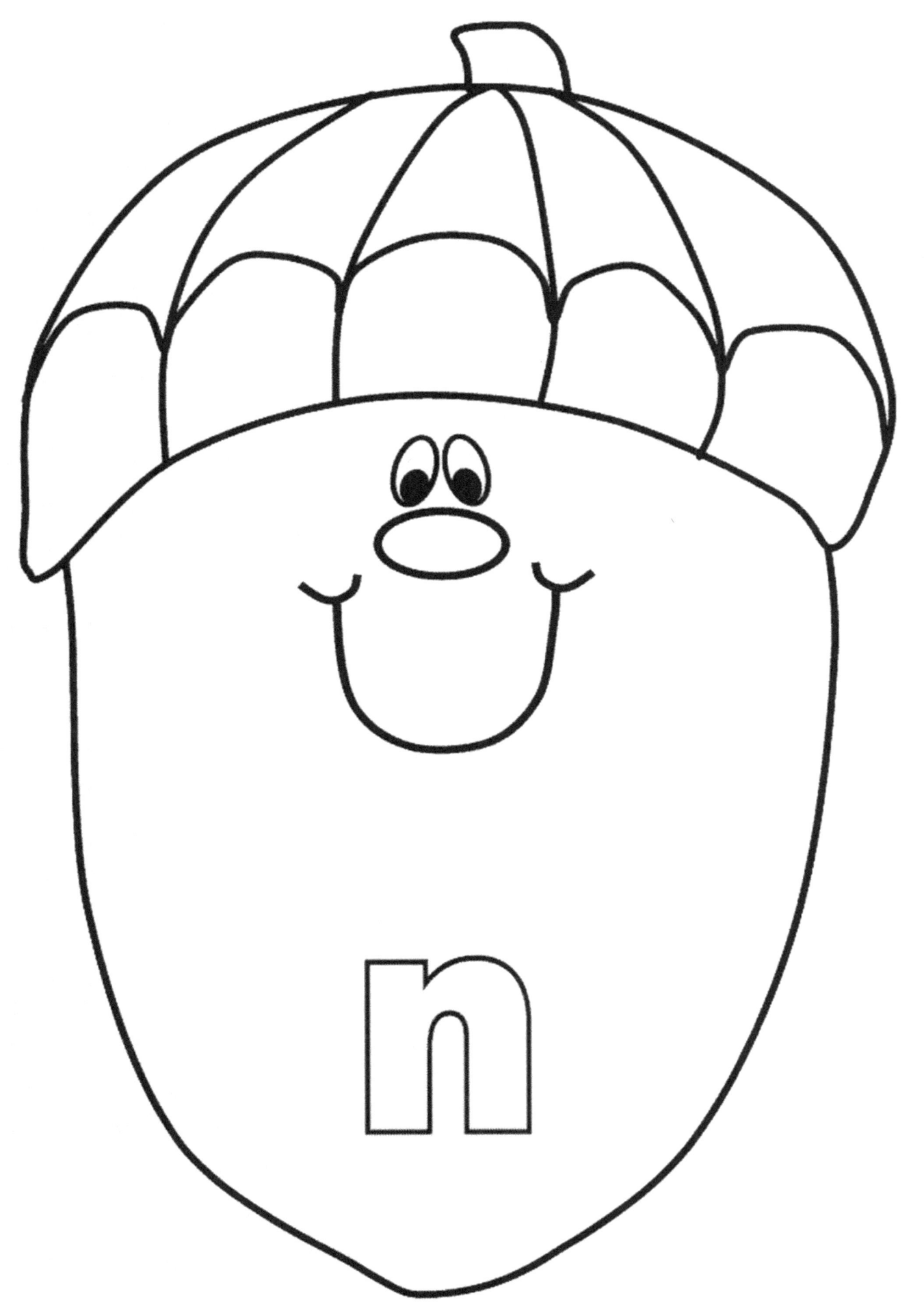

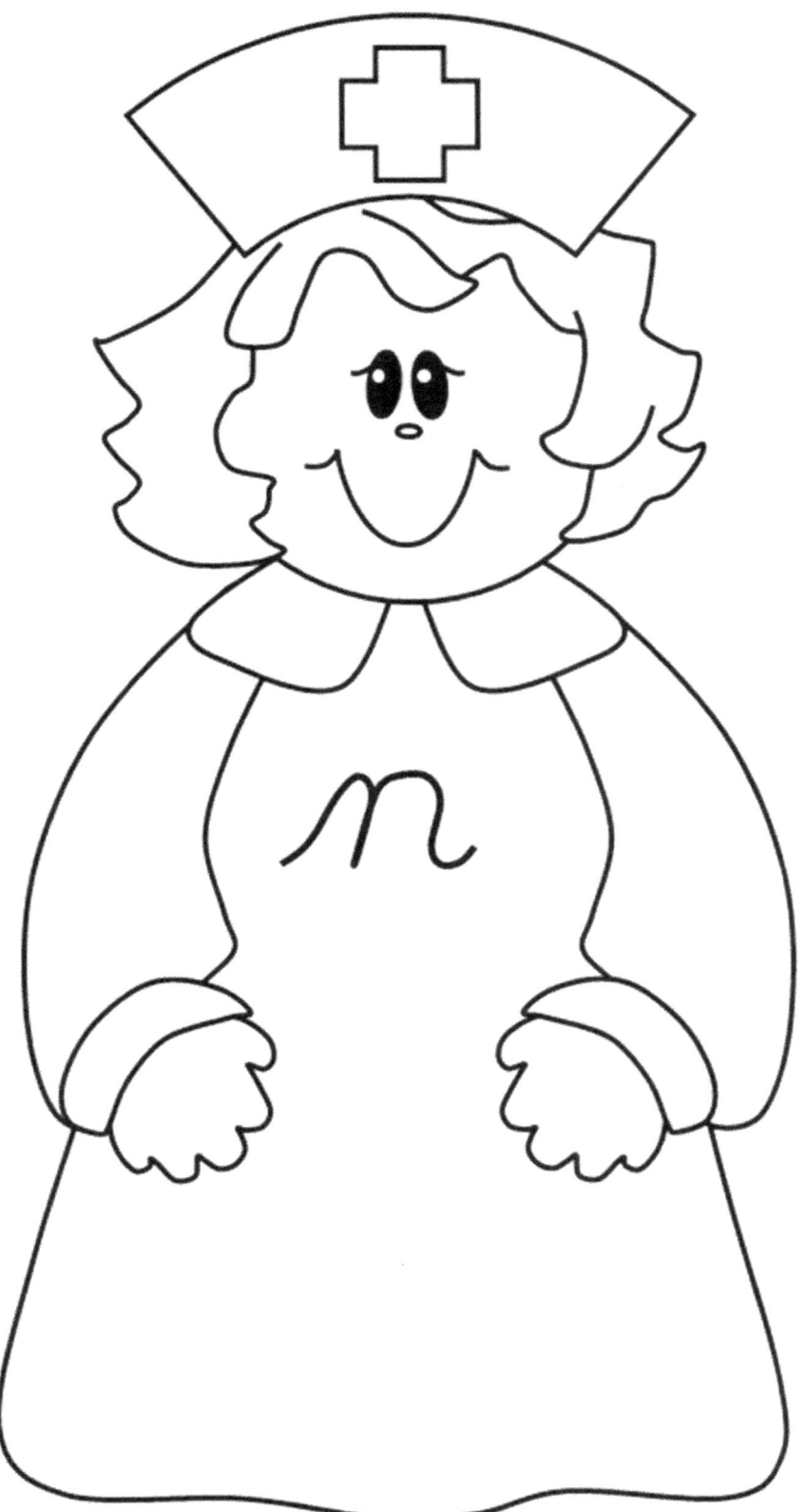

Trace the steps for making the letter n on the following line.

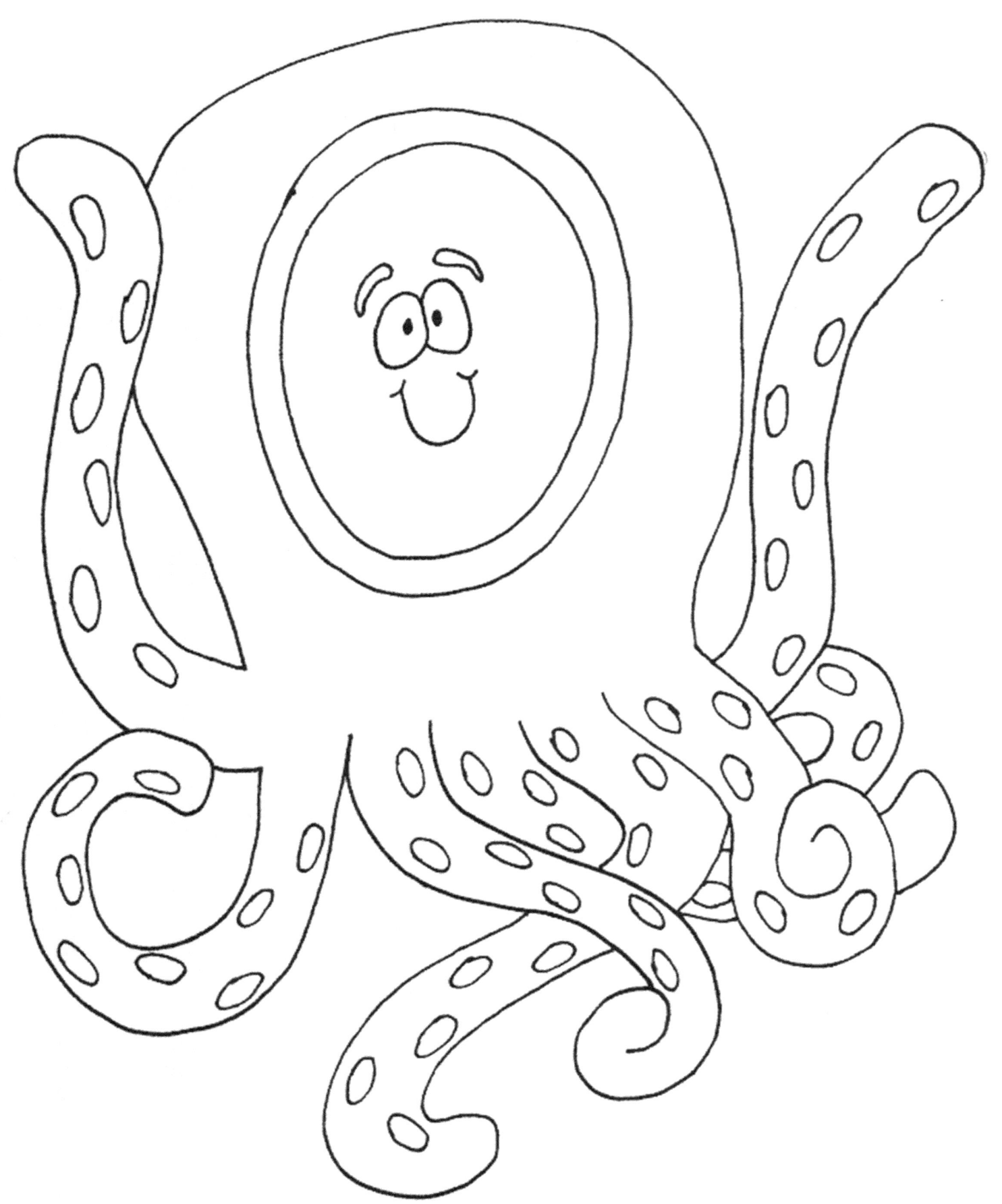

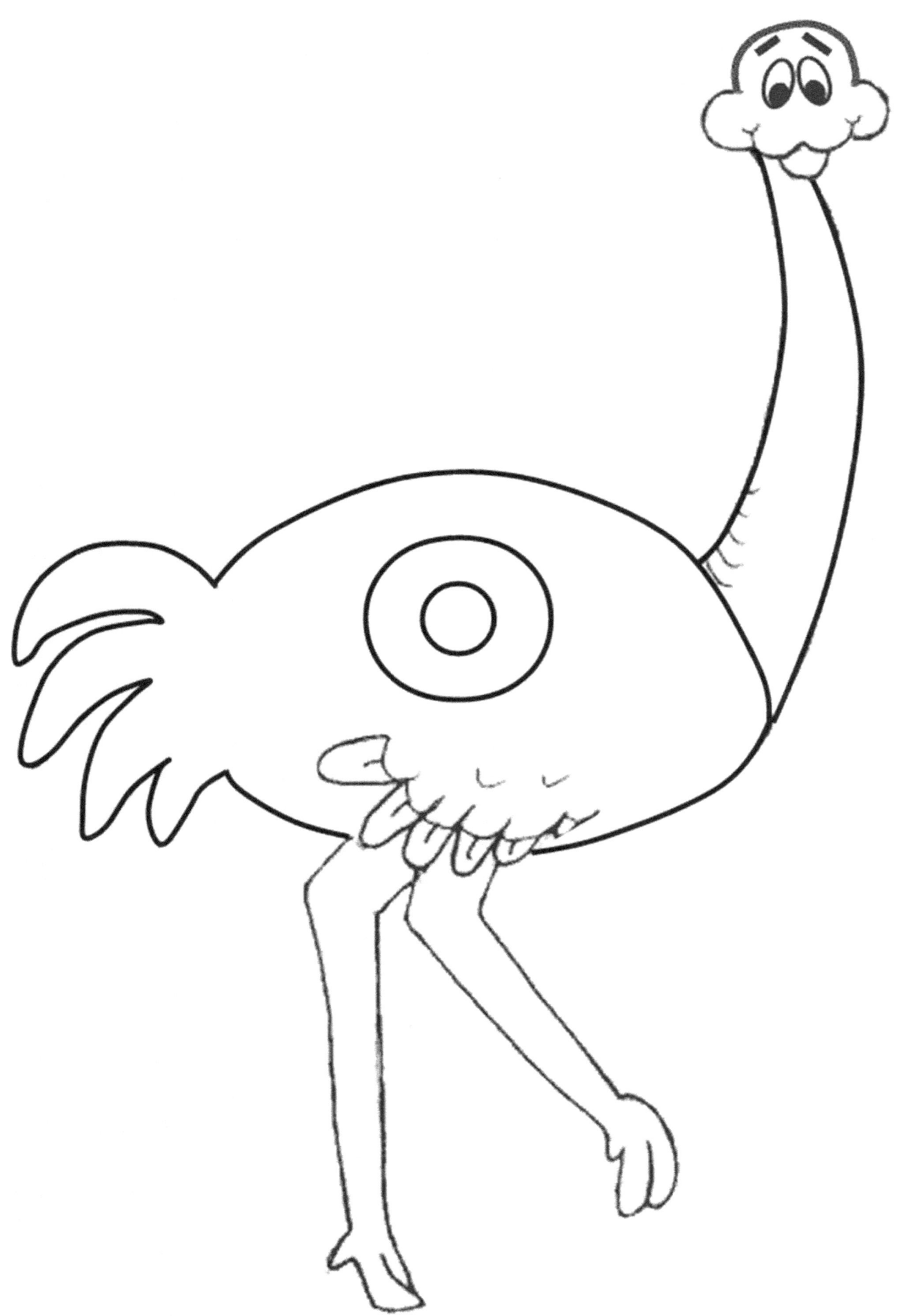

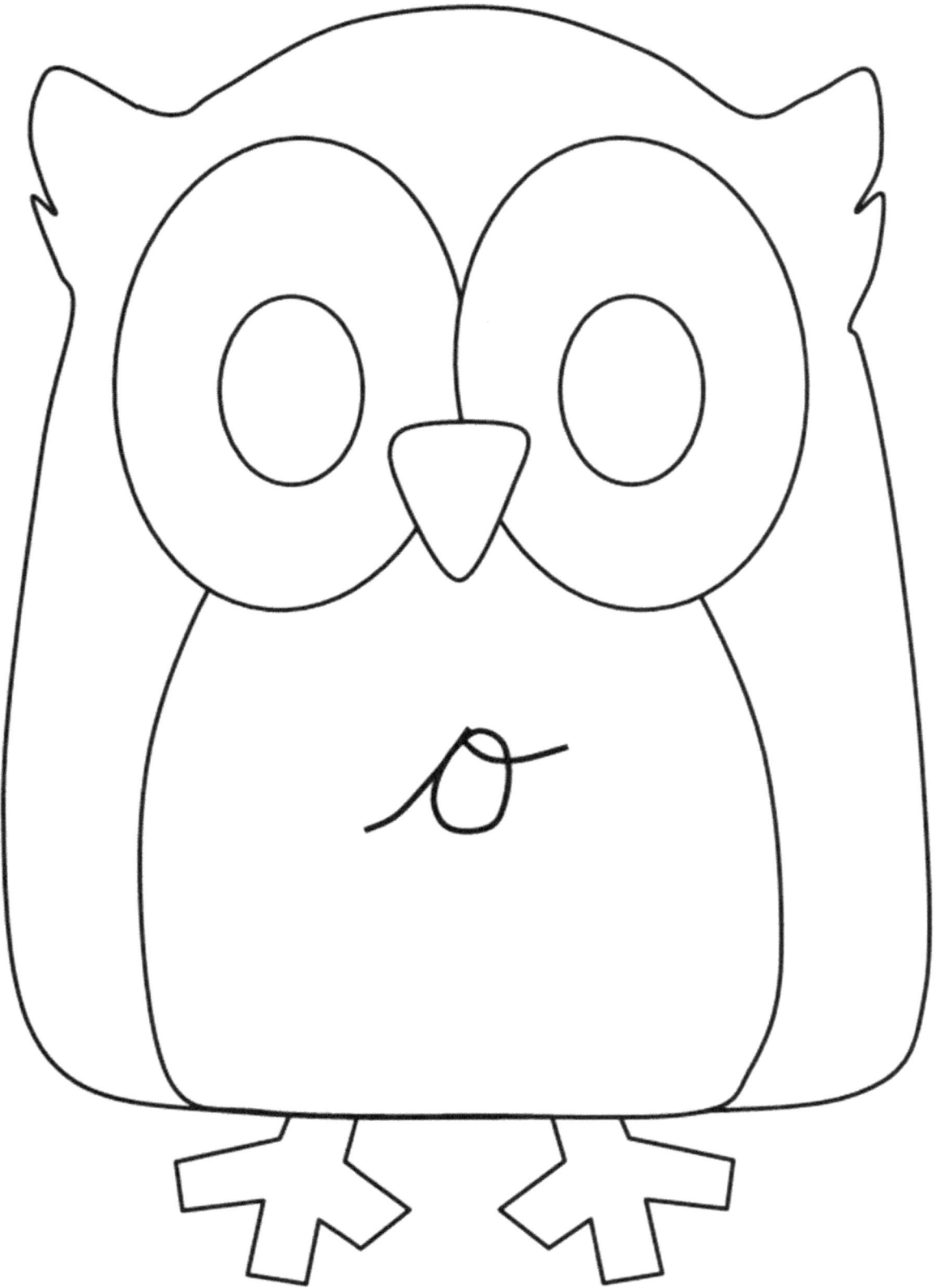

Trace the steps for making the letter o on the following line.

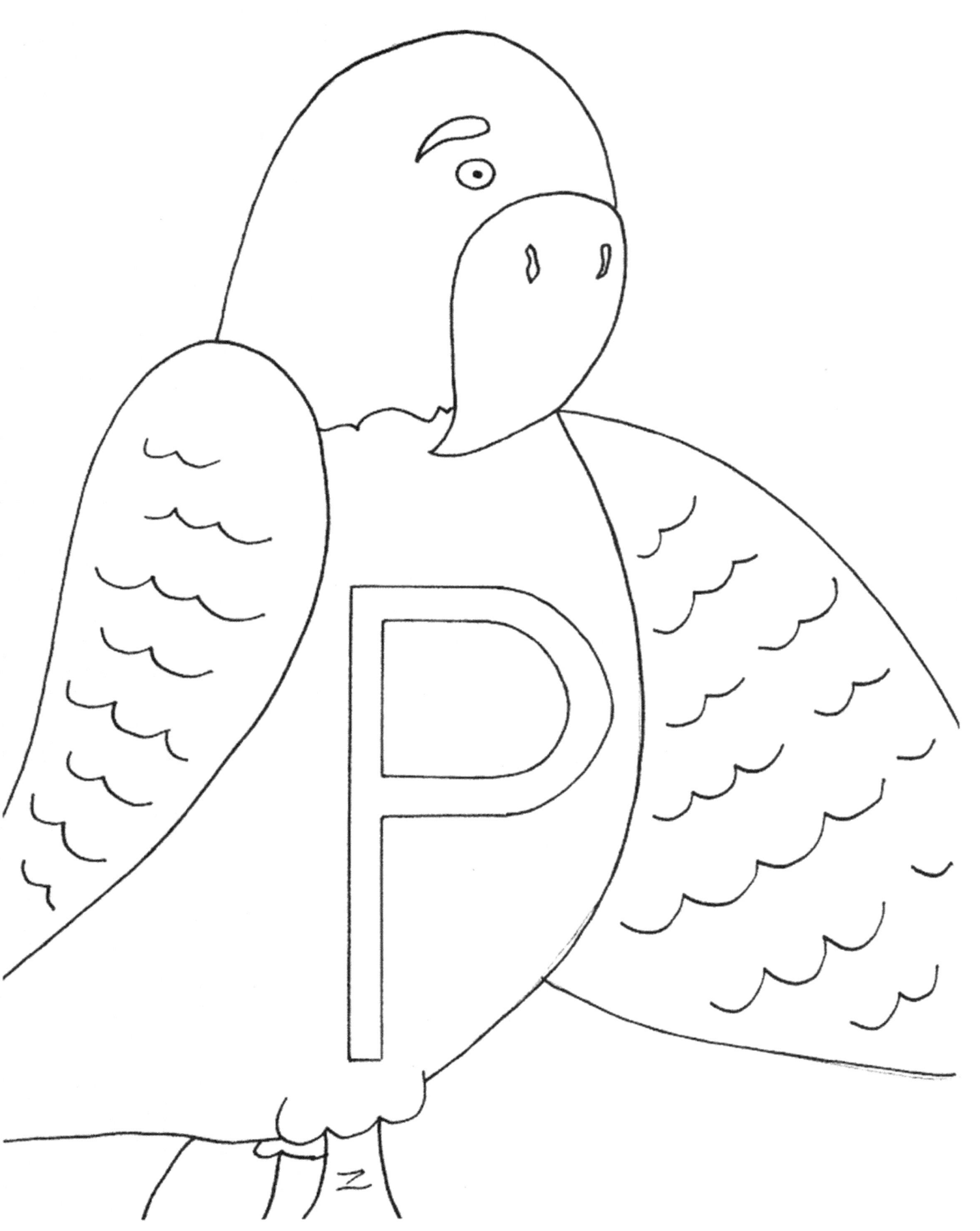

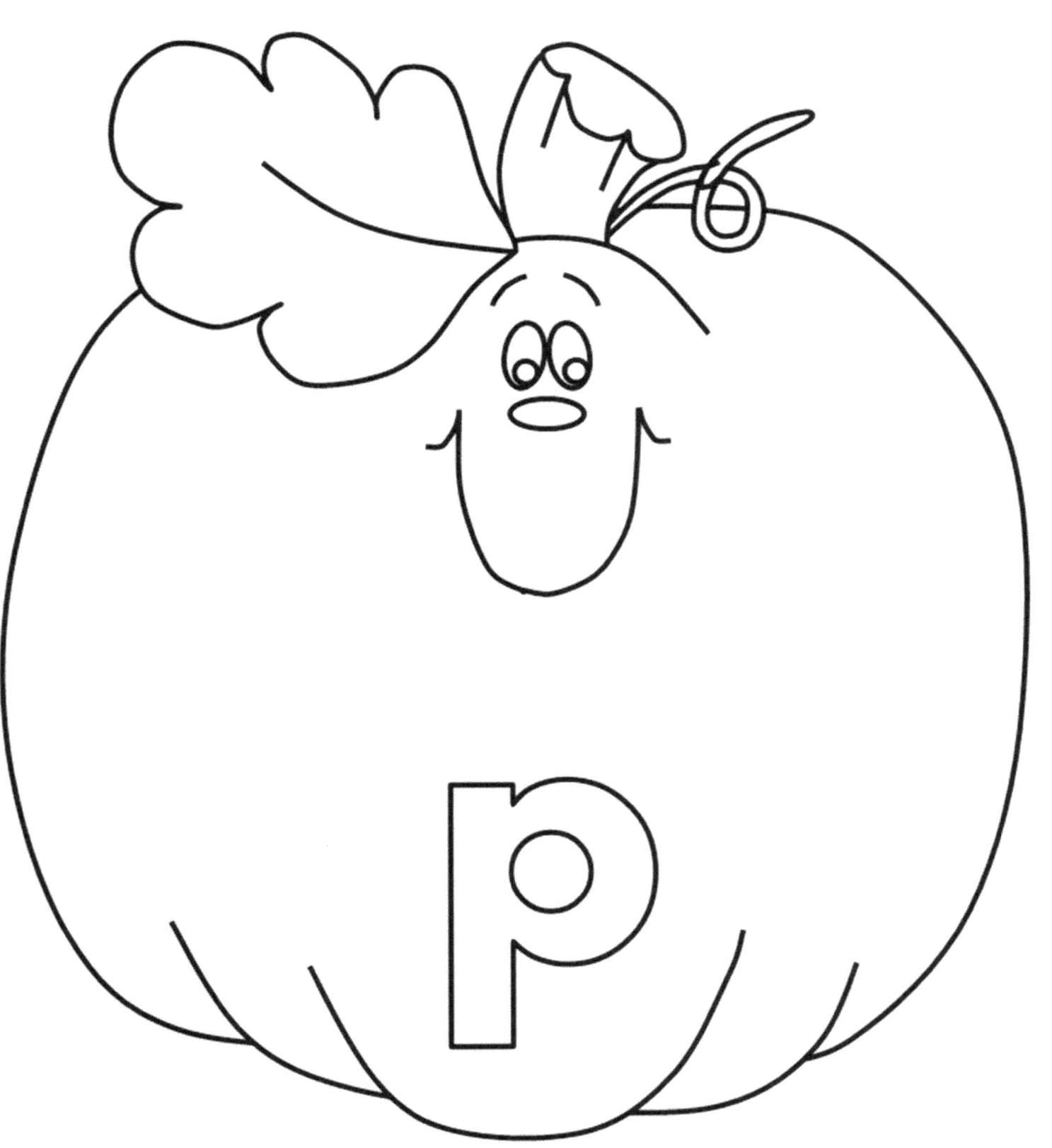

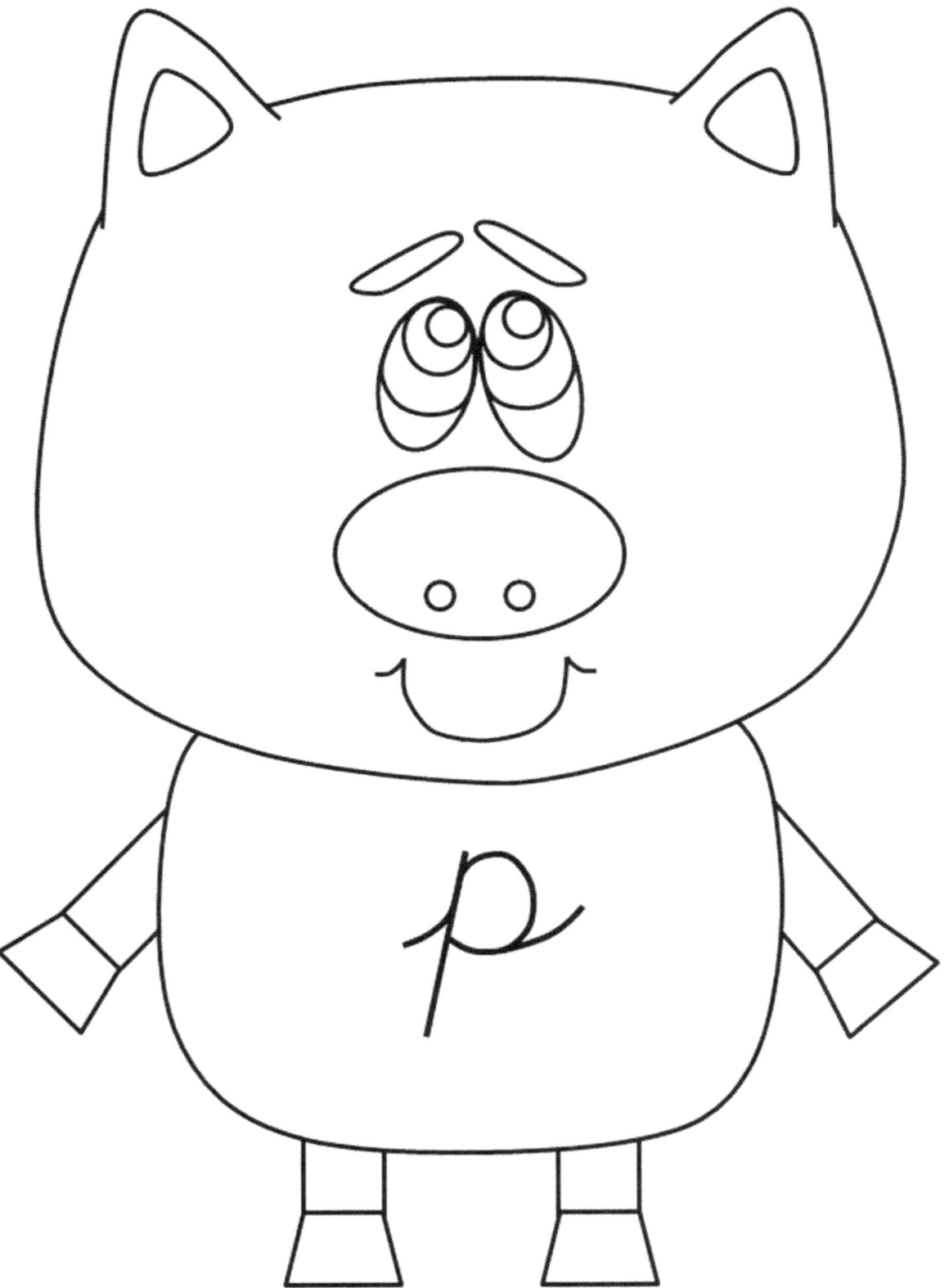

Trace the steps for making the letter p on the following line.

p    p    p    p    p    pp

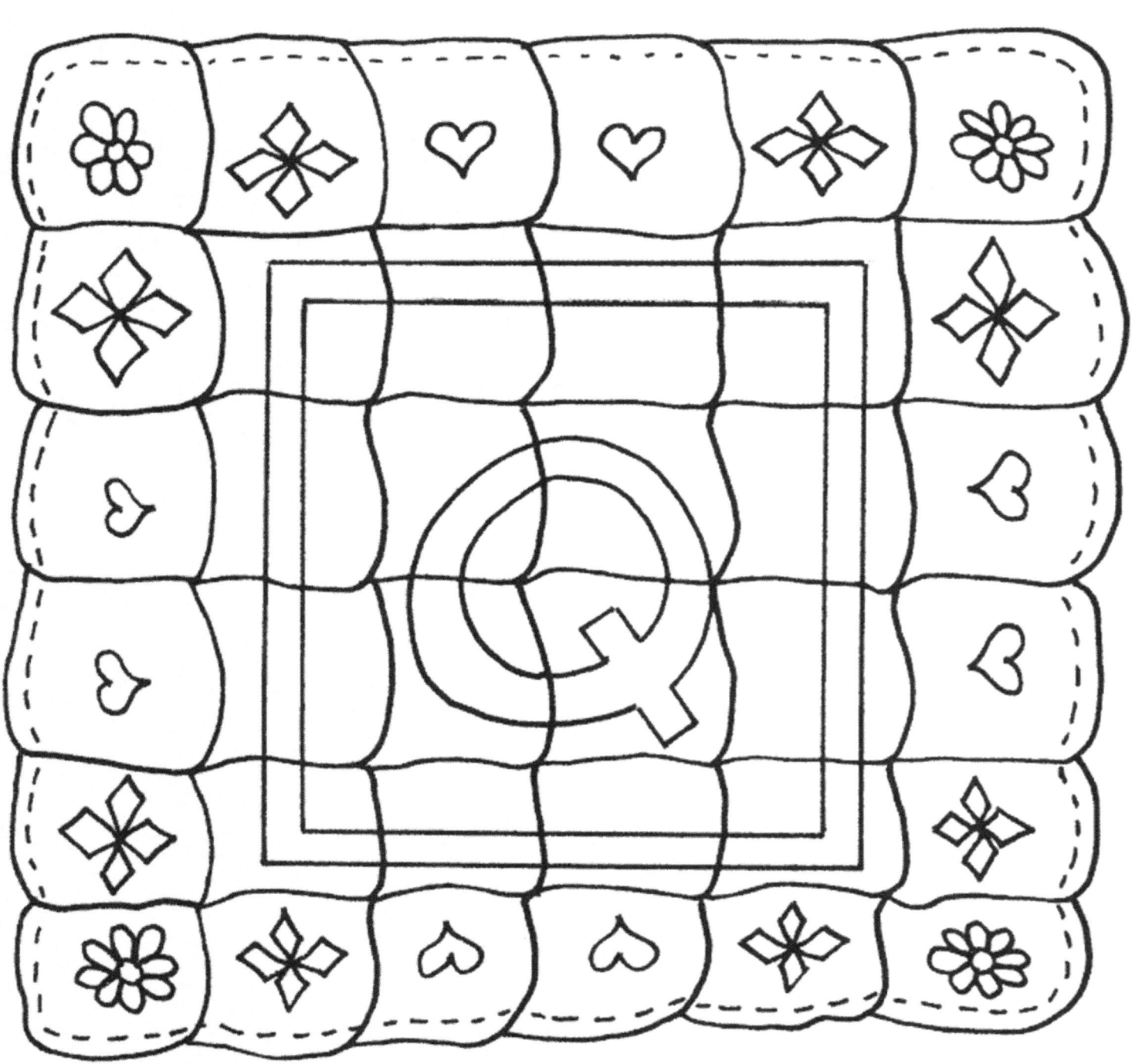

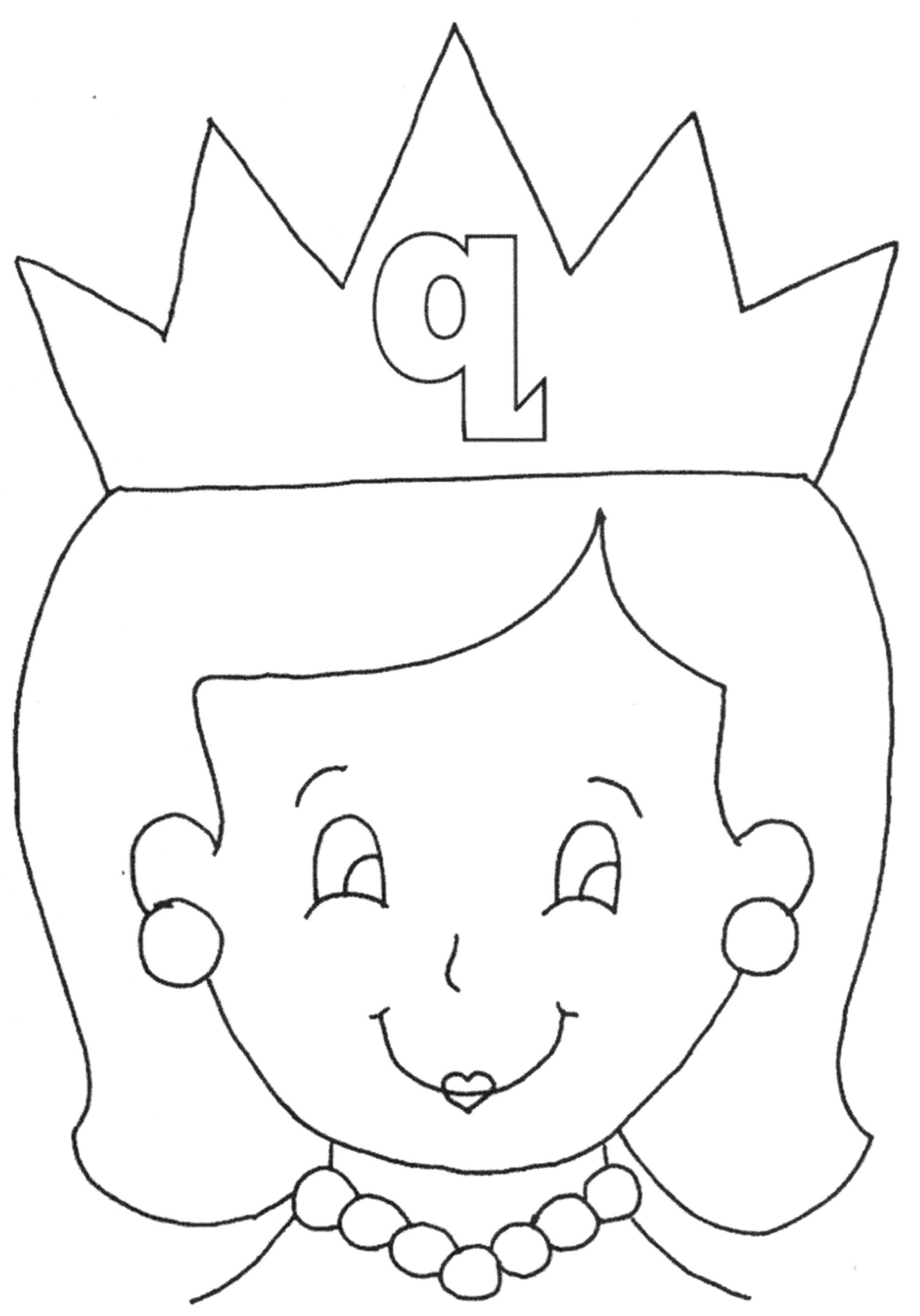

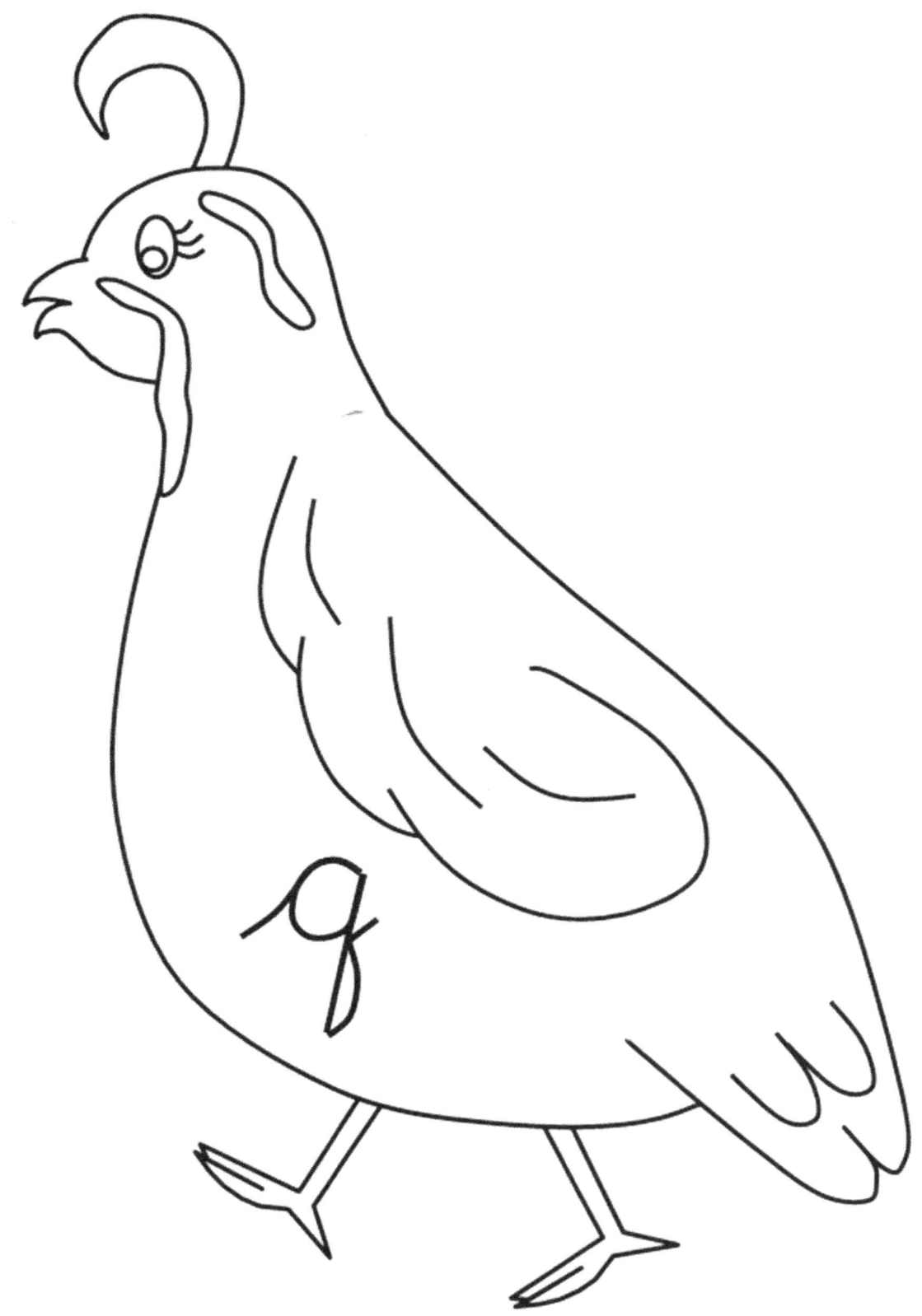

Trace the steps for making the letter q on the following line.

_q_ _q_ _q_ _q_ _q_

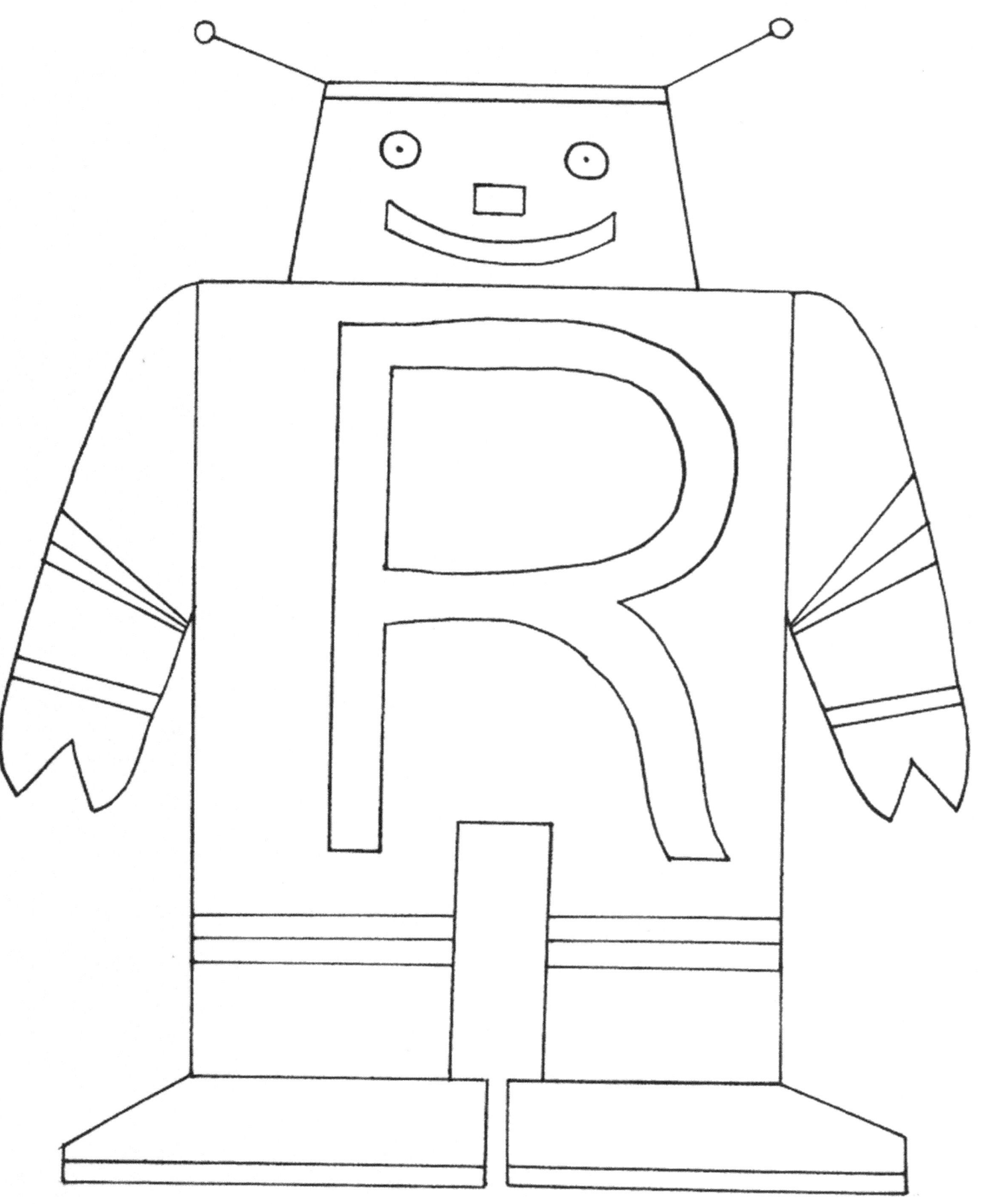

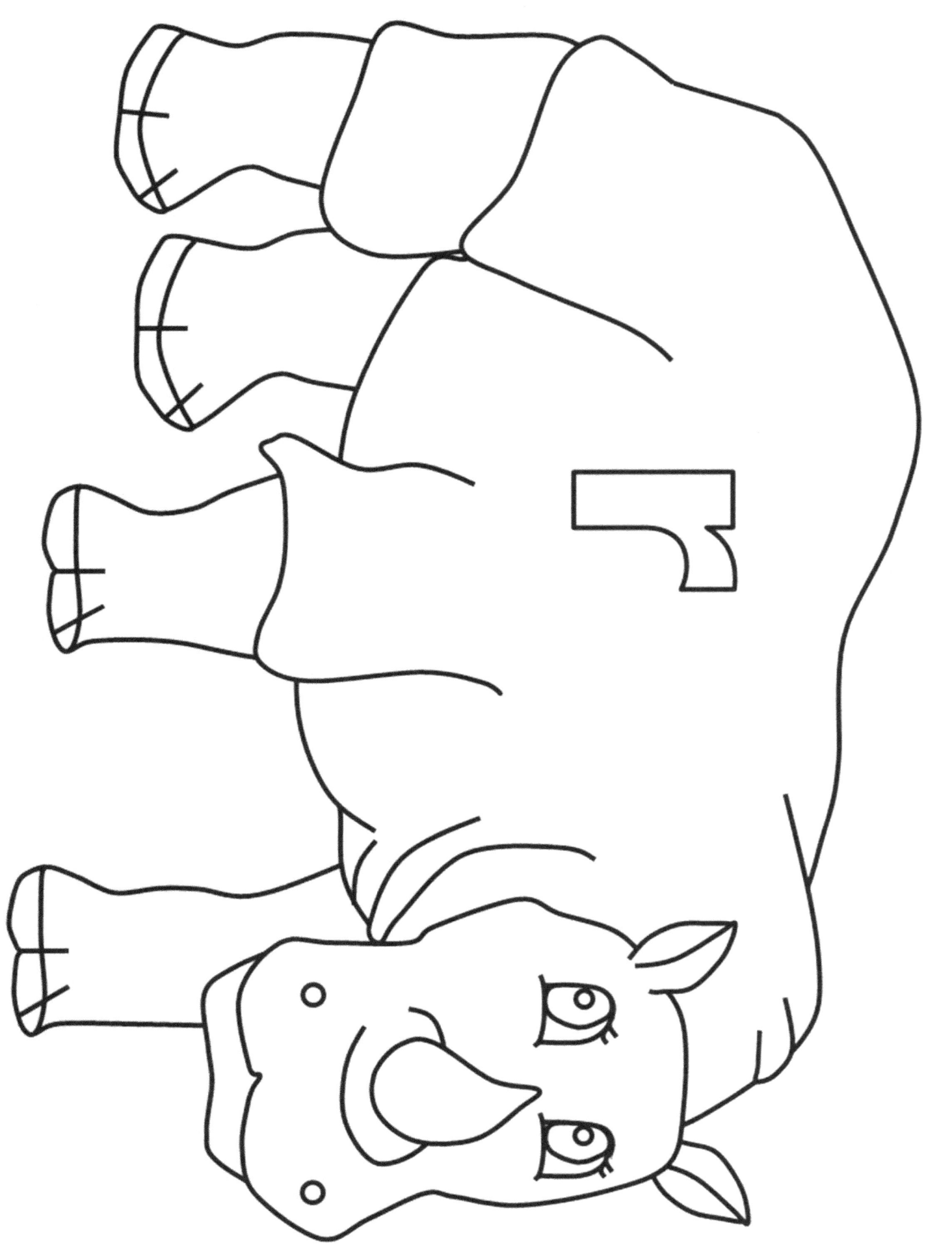

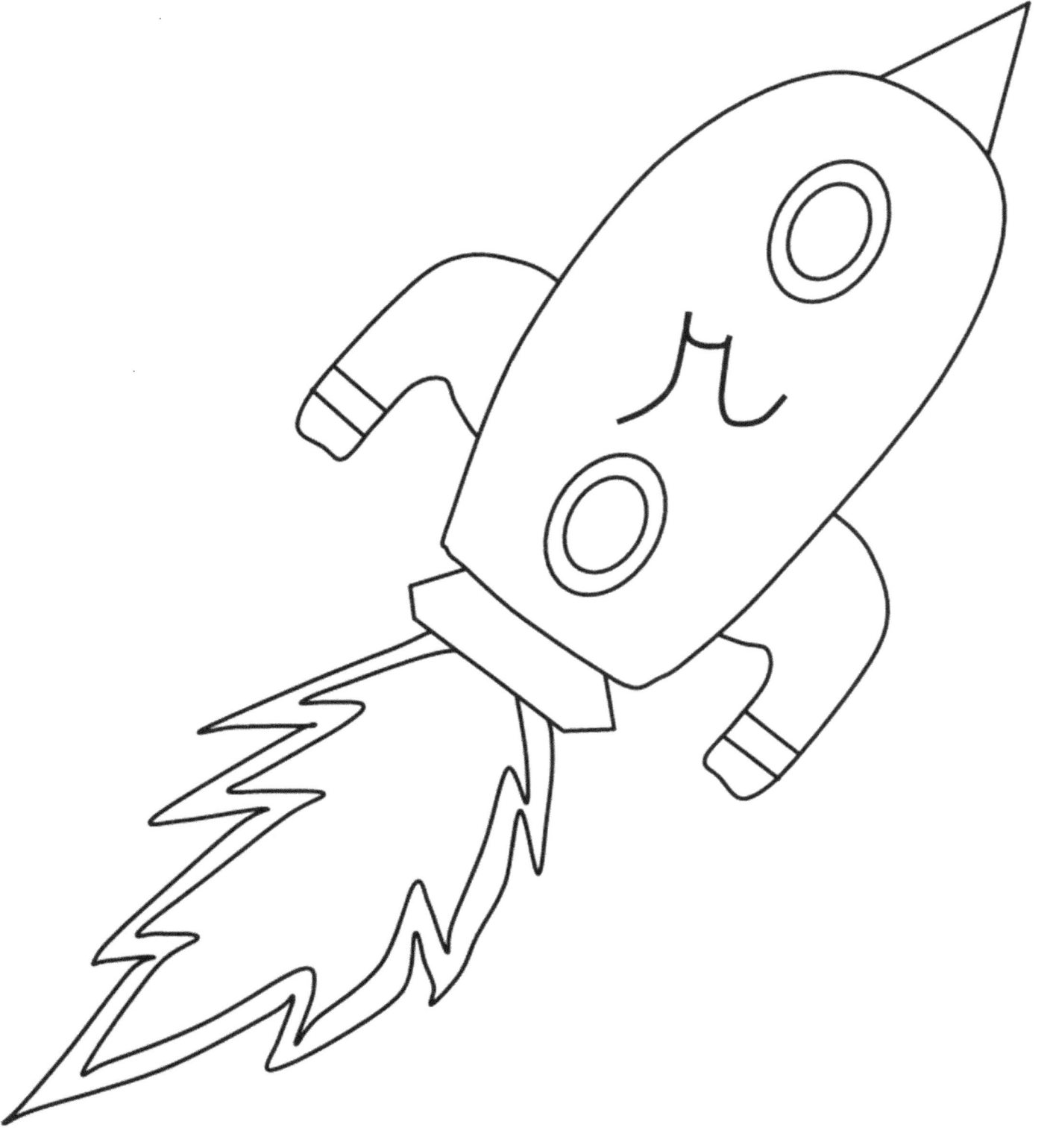

Trace the steps for making the letter r on the following line.

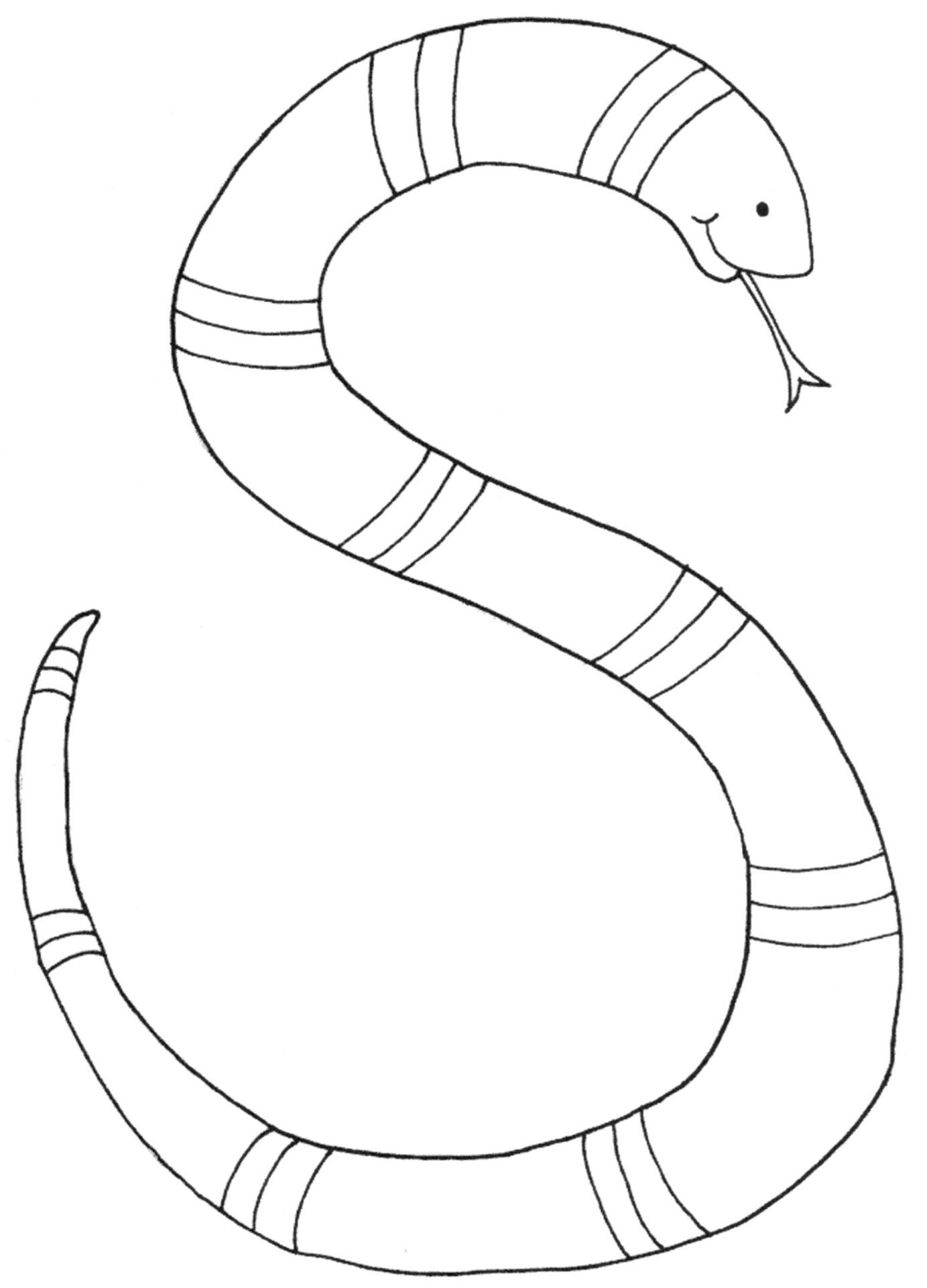

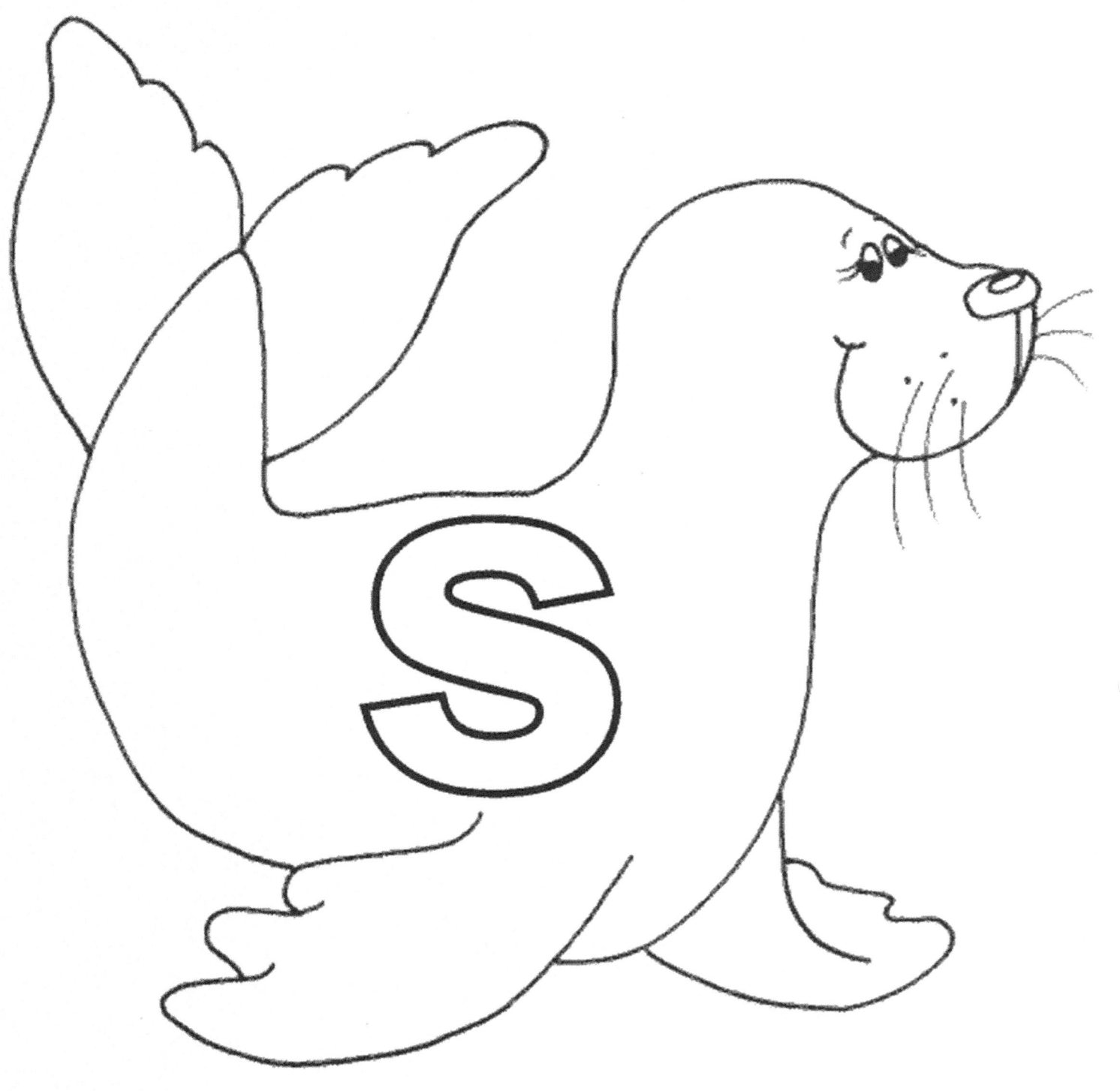

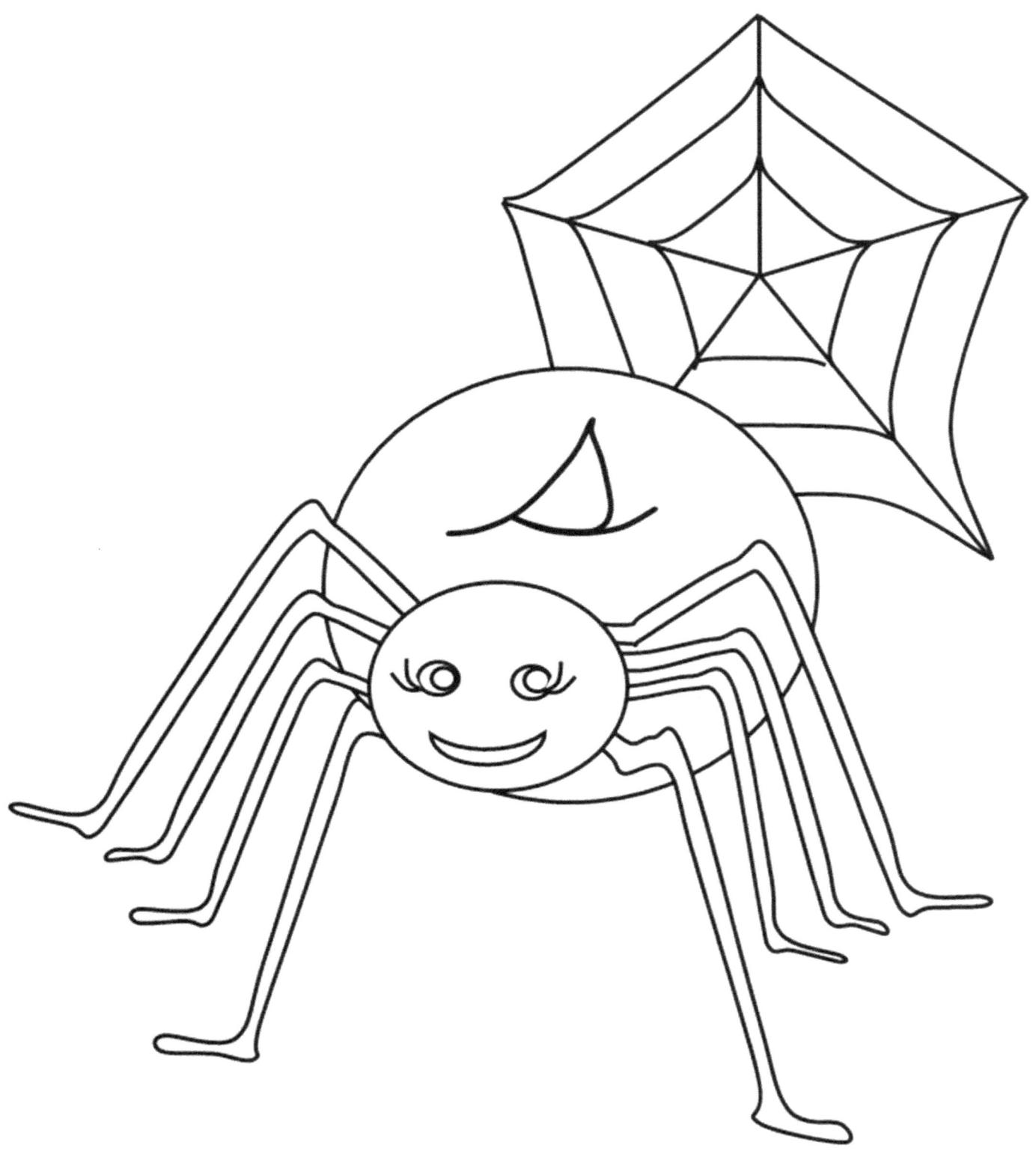

Trace the steps for making the letter s on the following line.

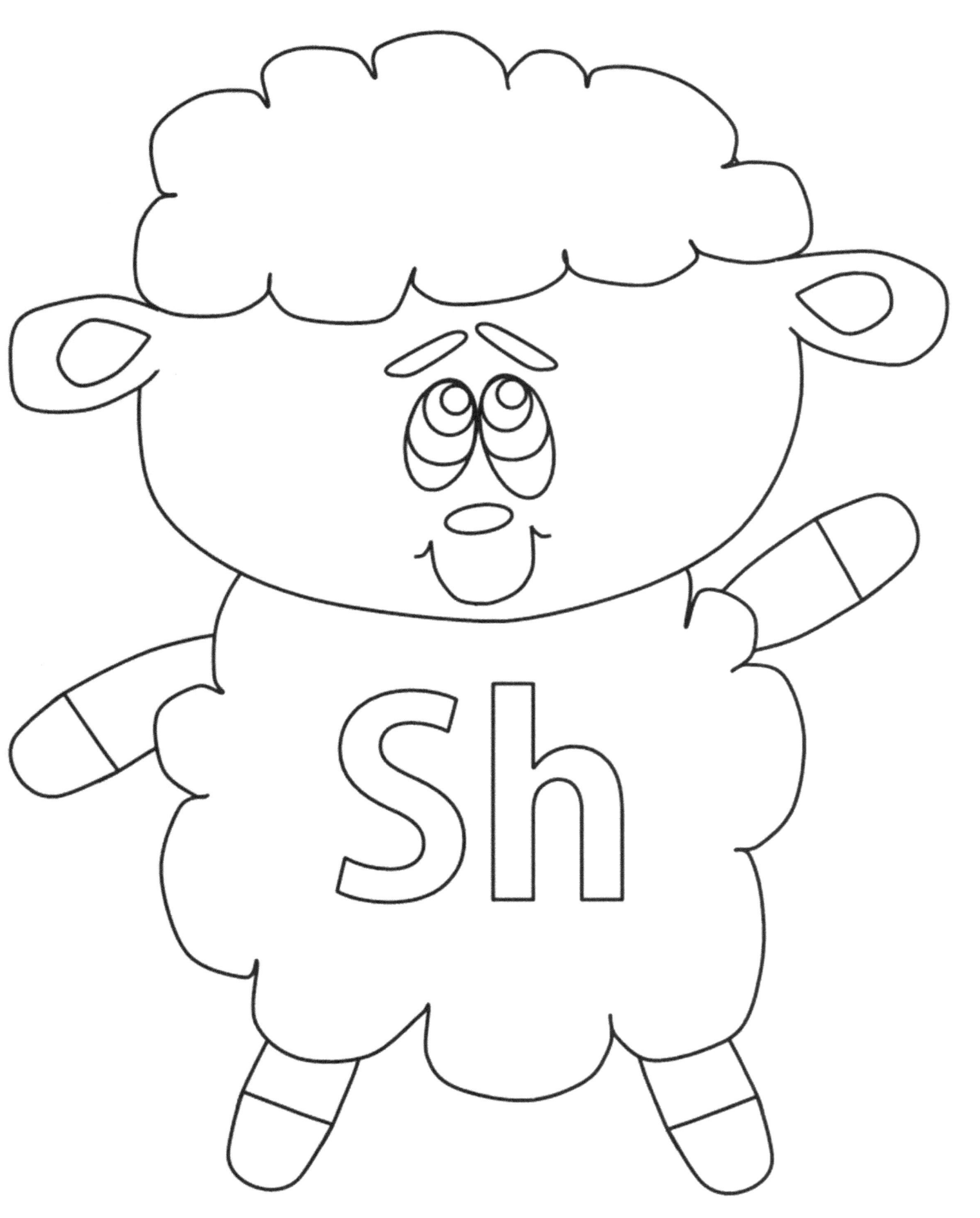

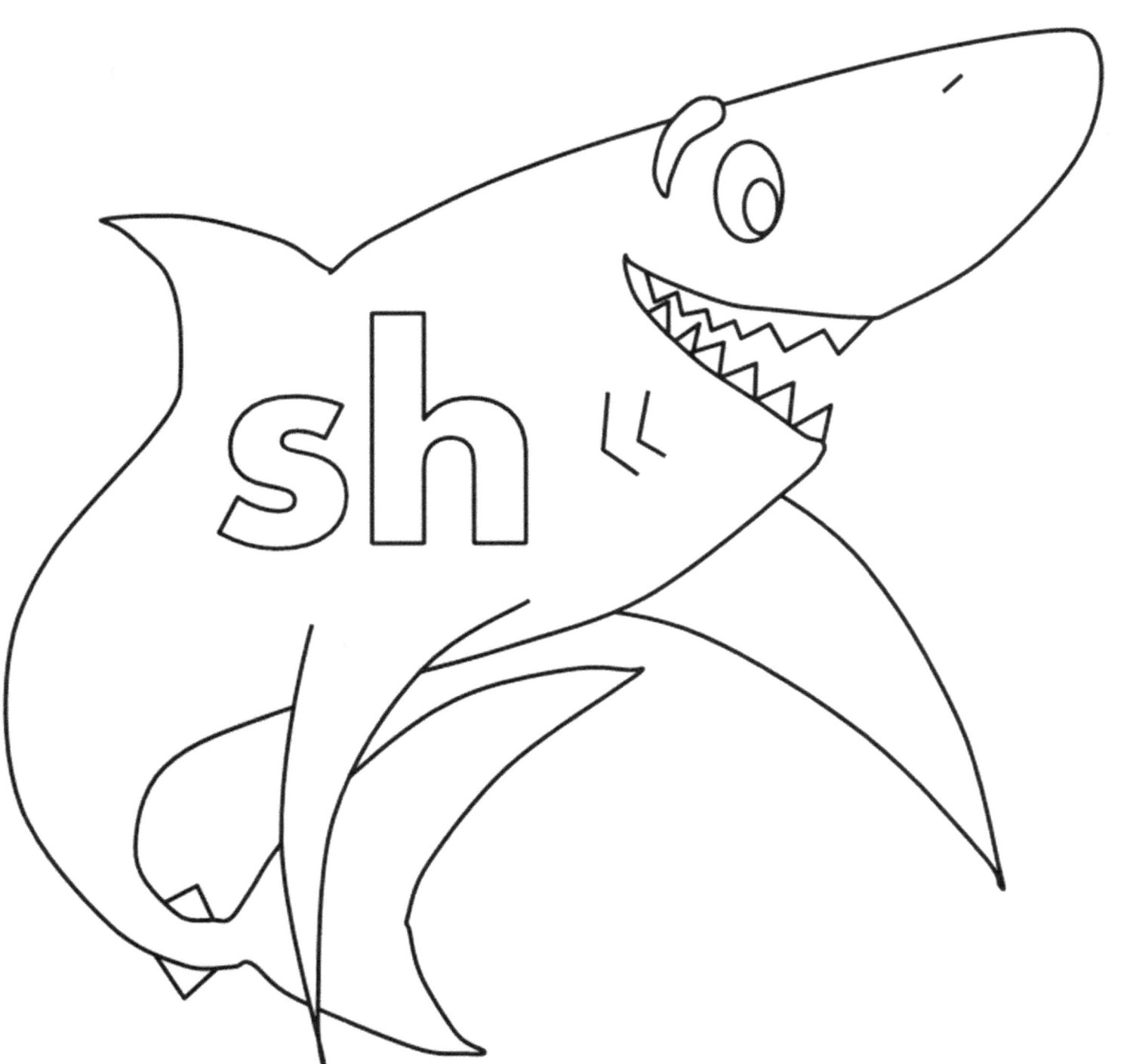

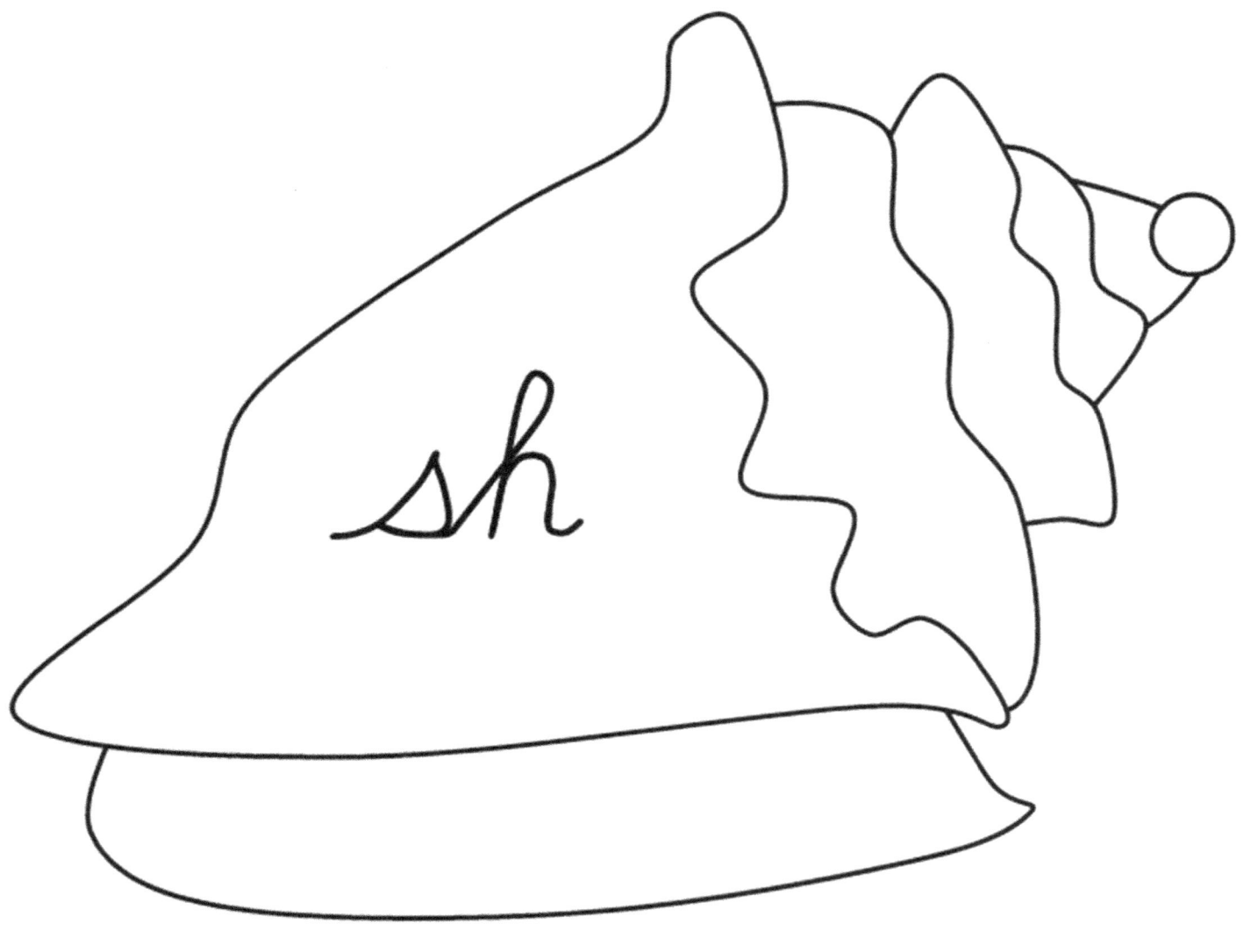

Trace the steps for making the letter sh on the following line.

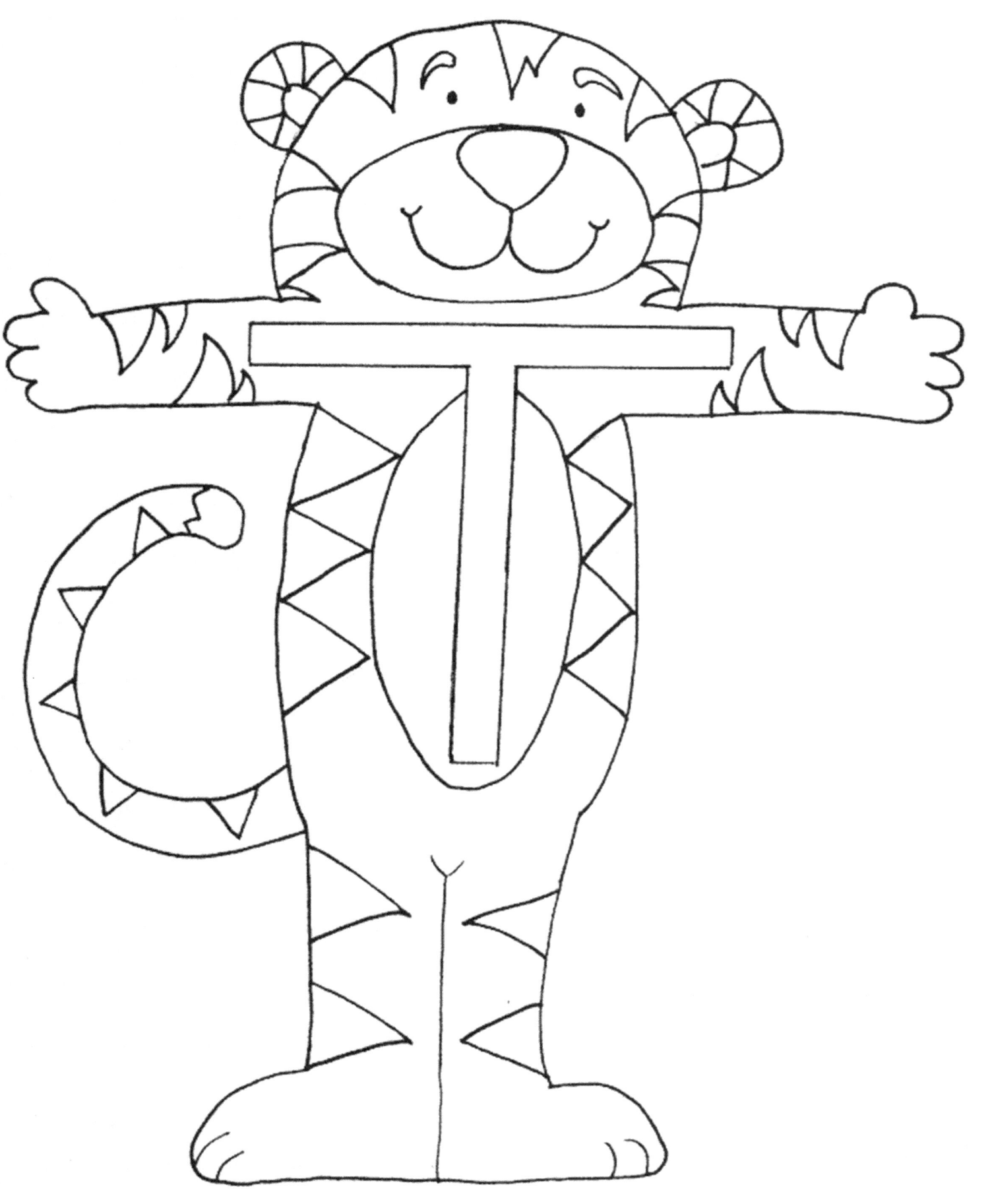

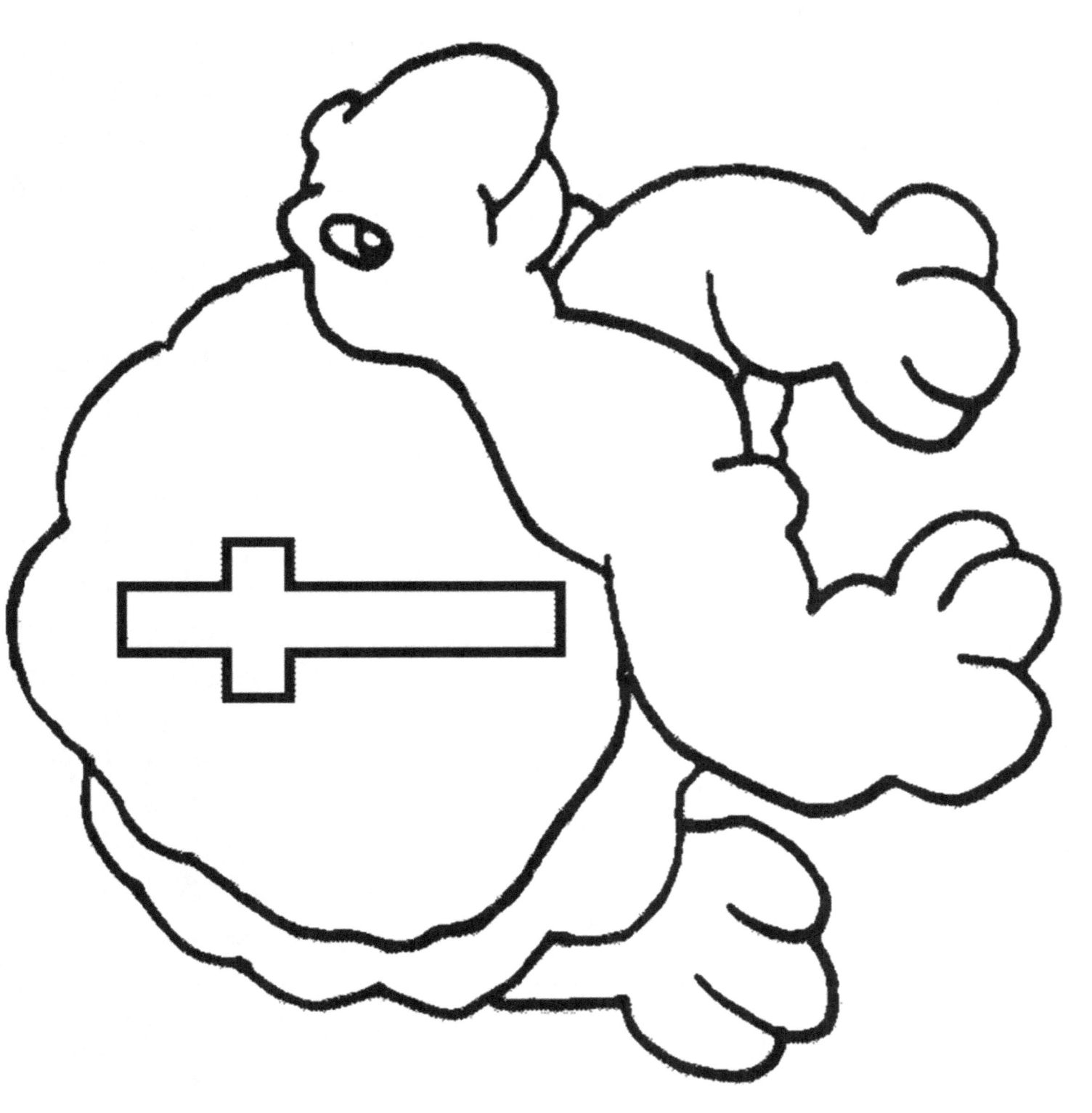

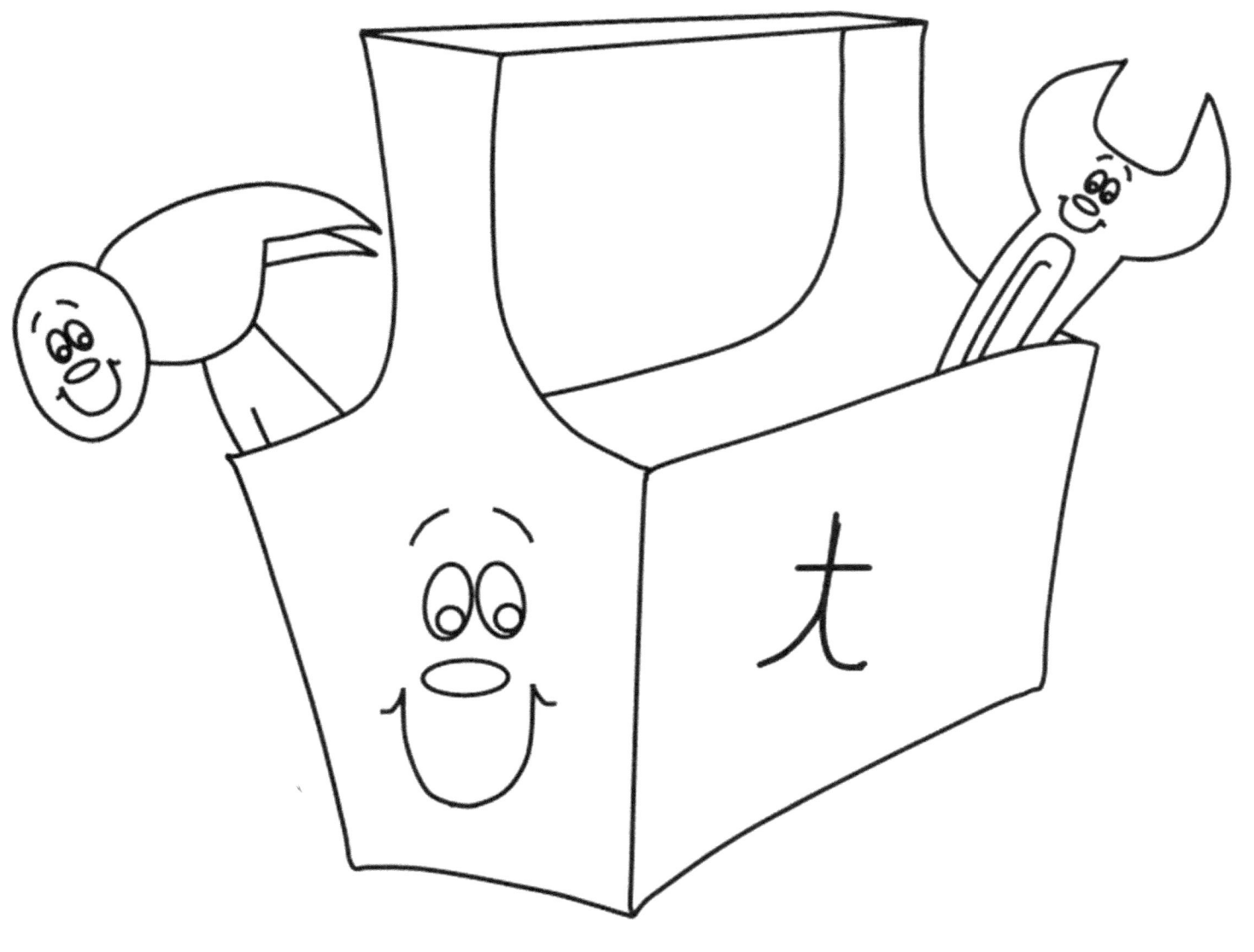

Trace the steps for making the letter t on the following line.

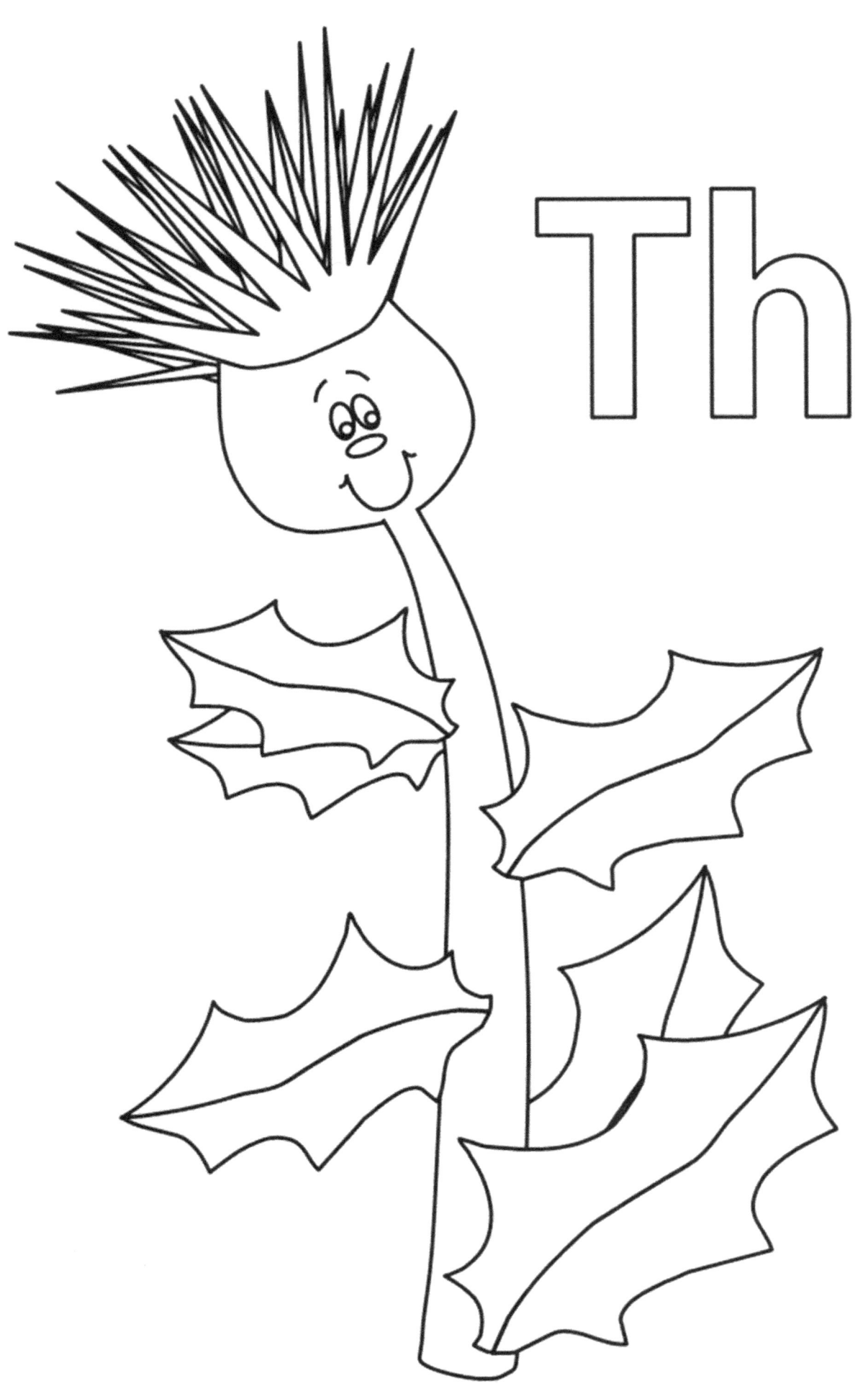

Th

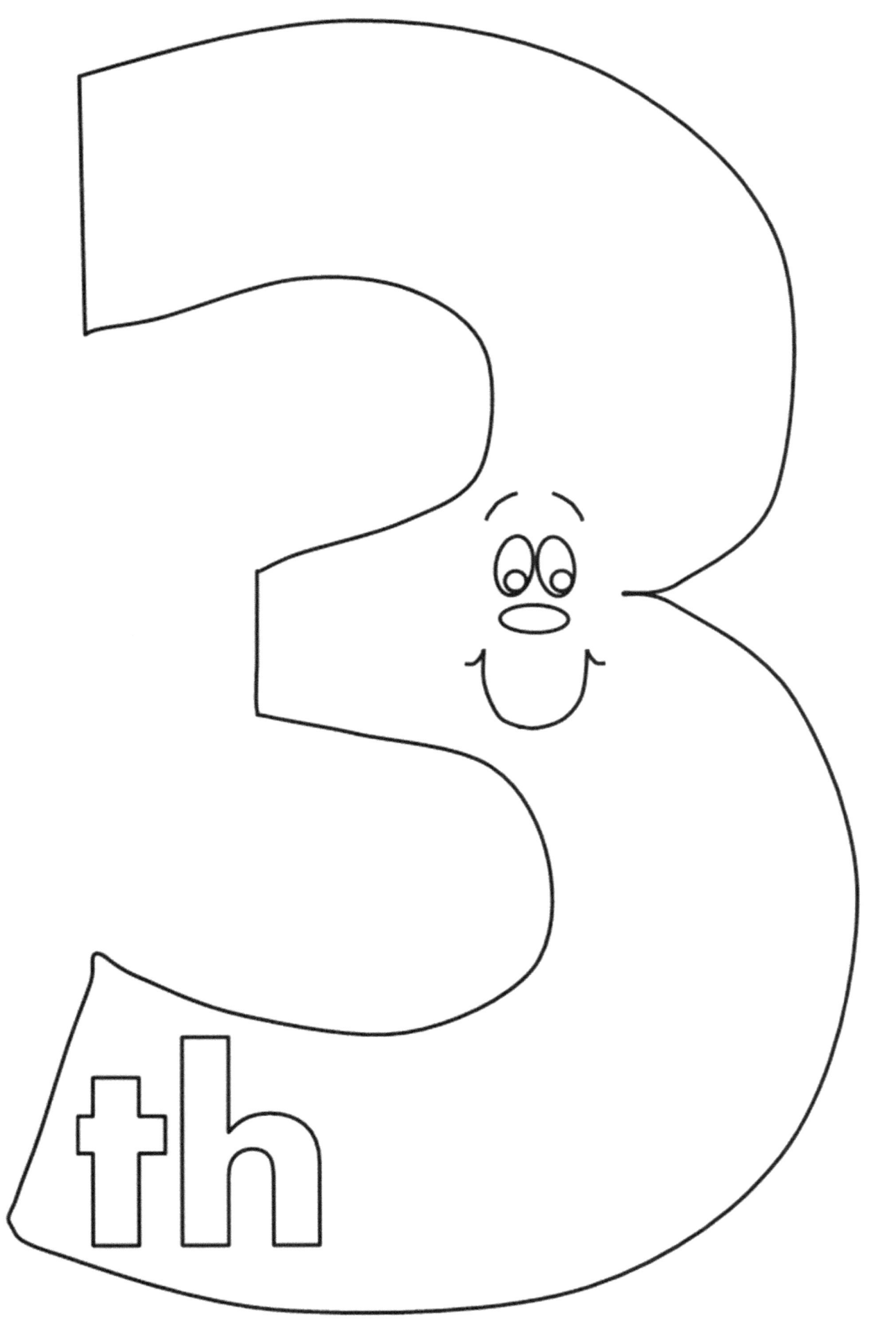

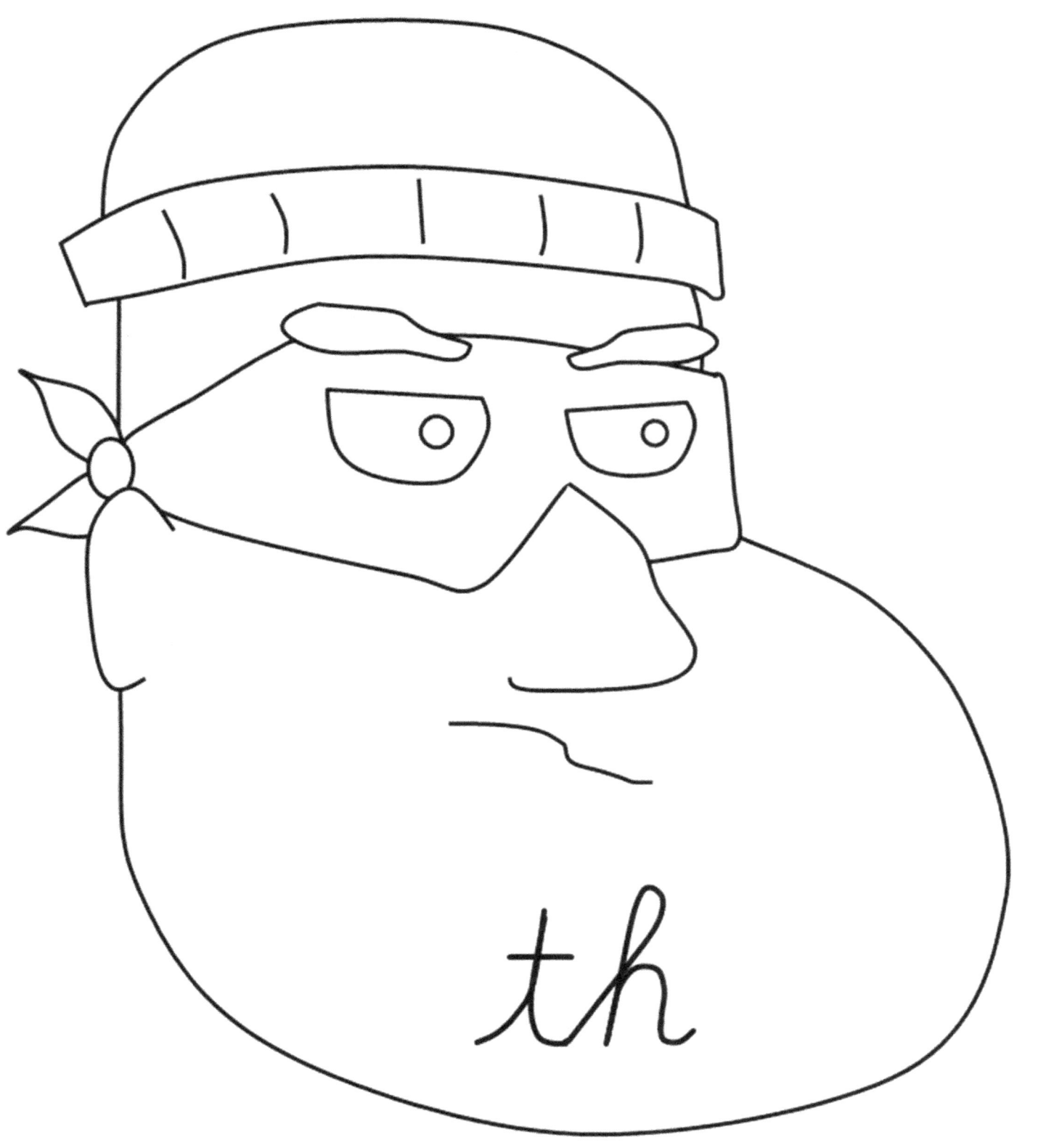

th

Trace the steps for making the letter th on the following line.

th th th th th

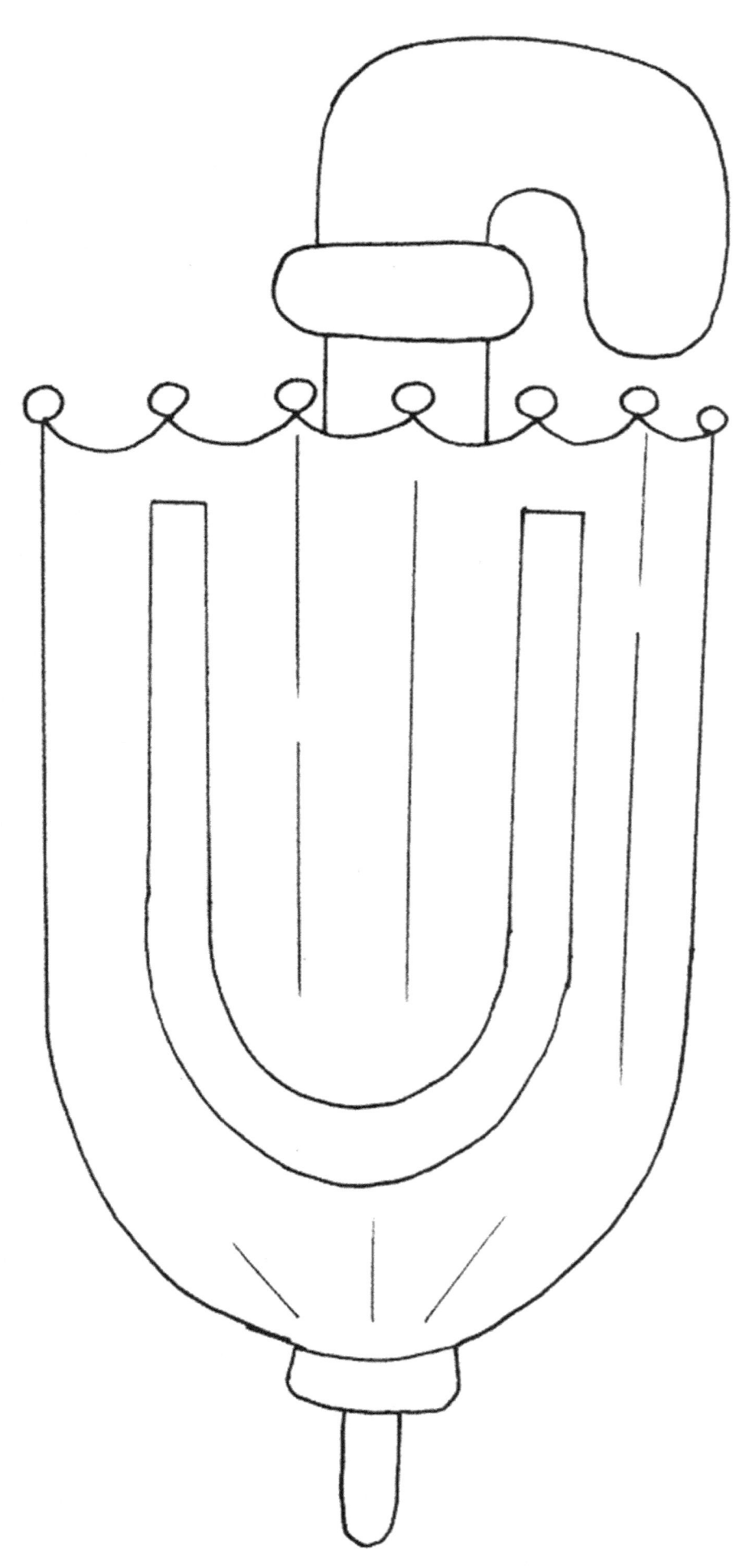

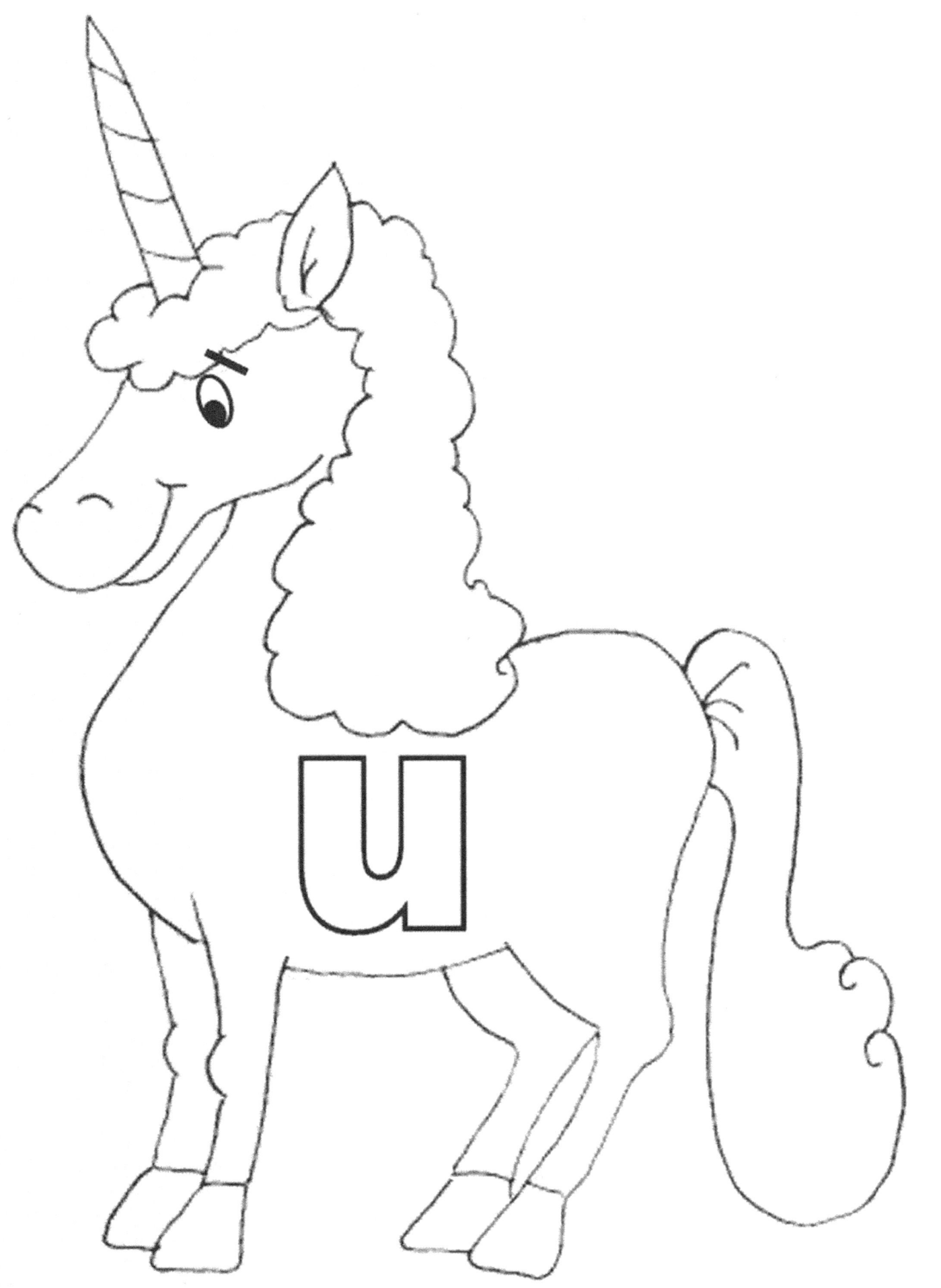

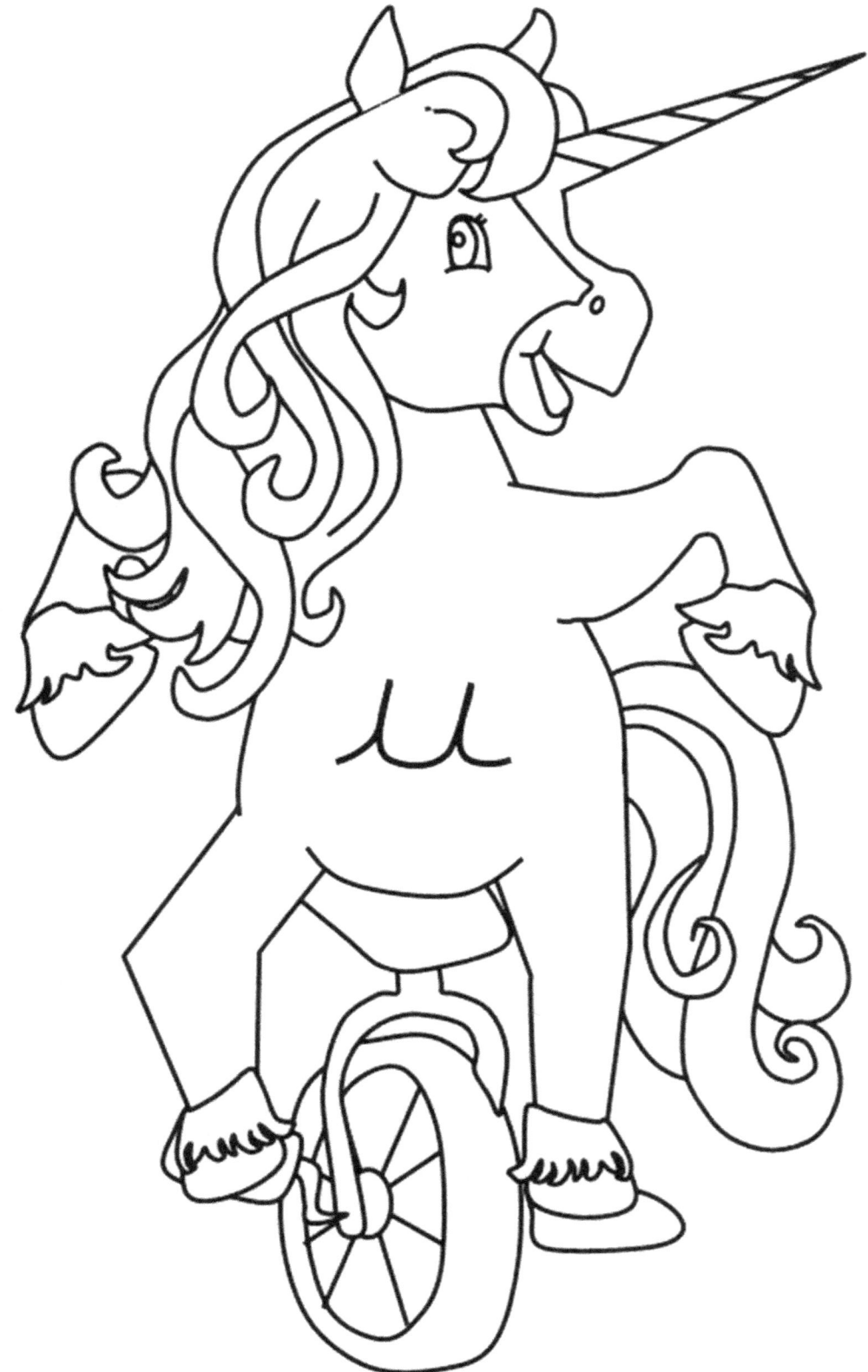

Trace the steps for making the letter u on the following line.

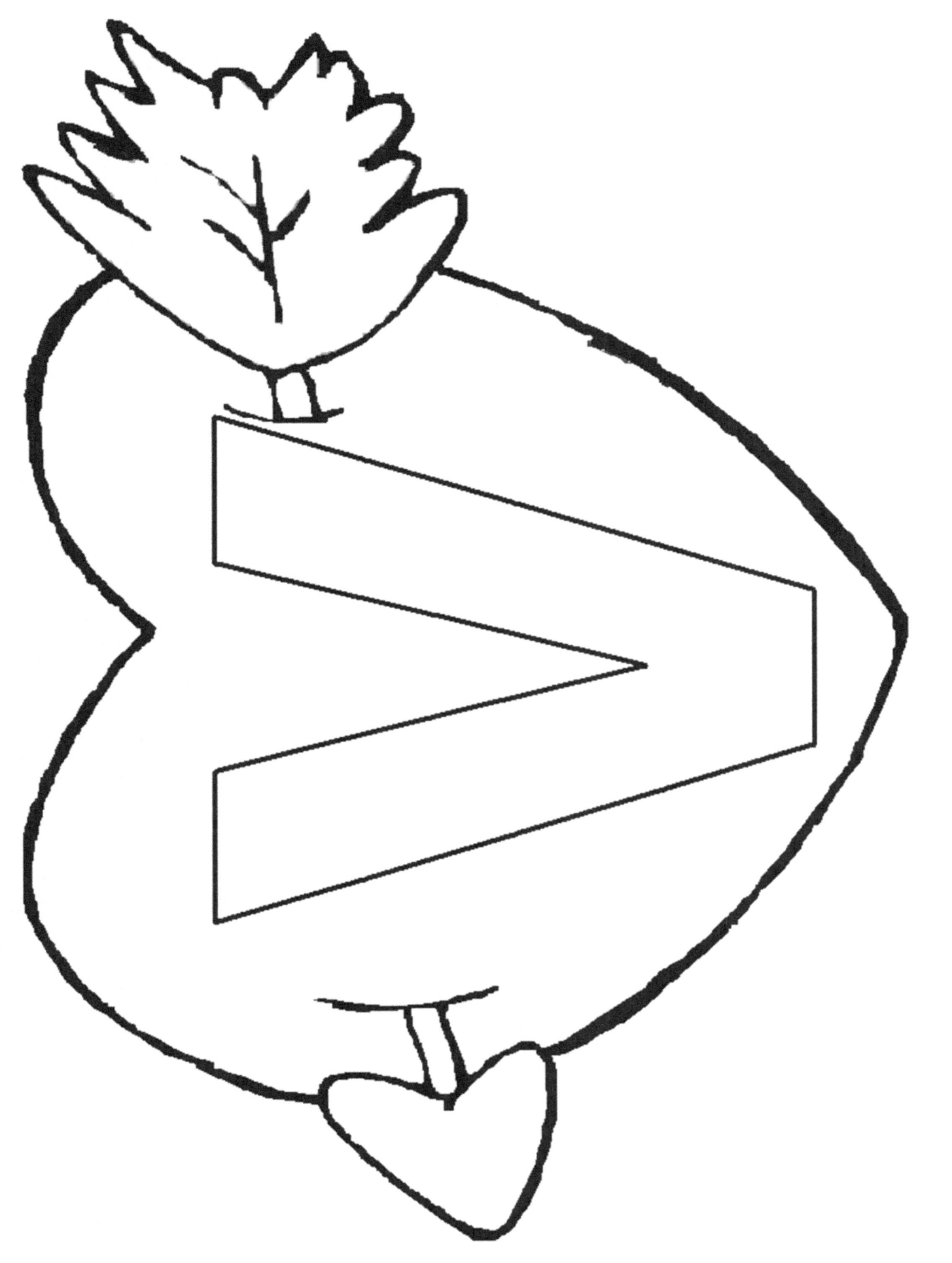

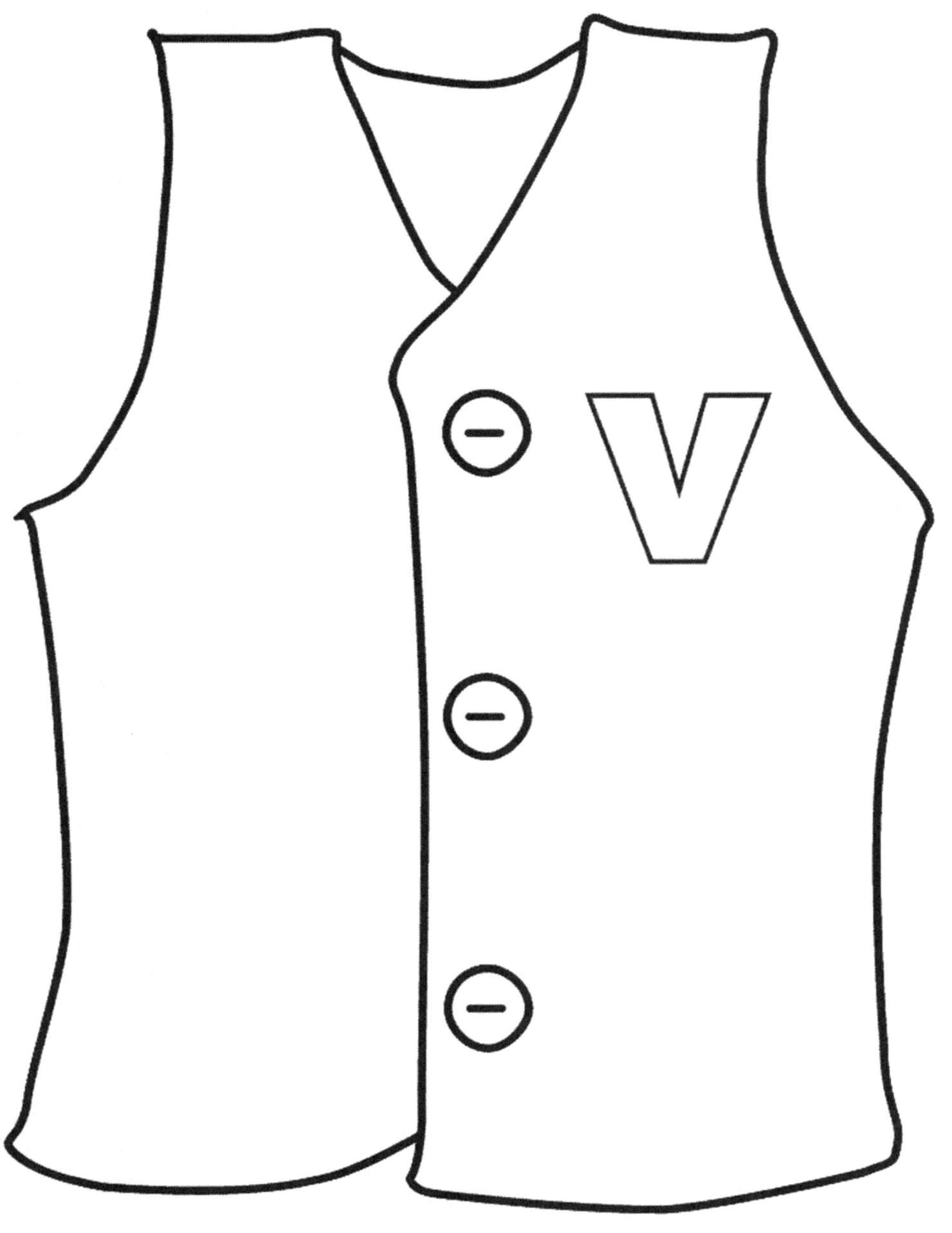

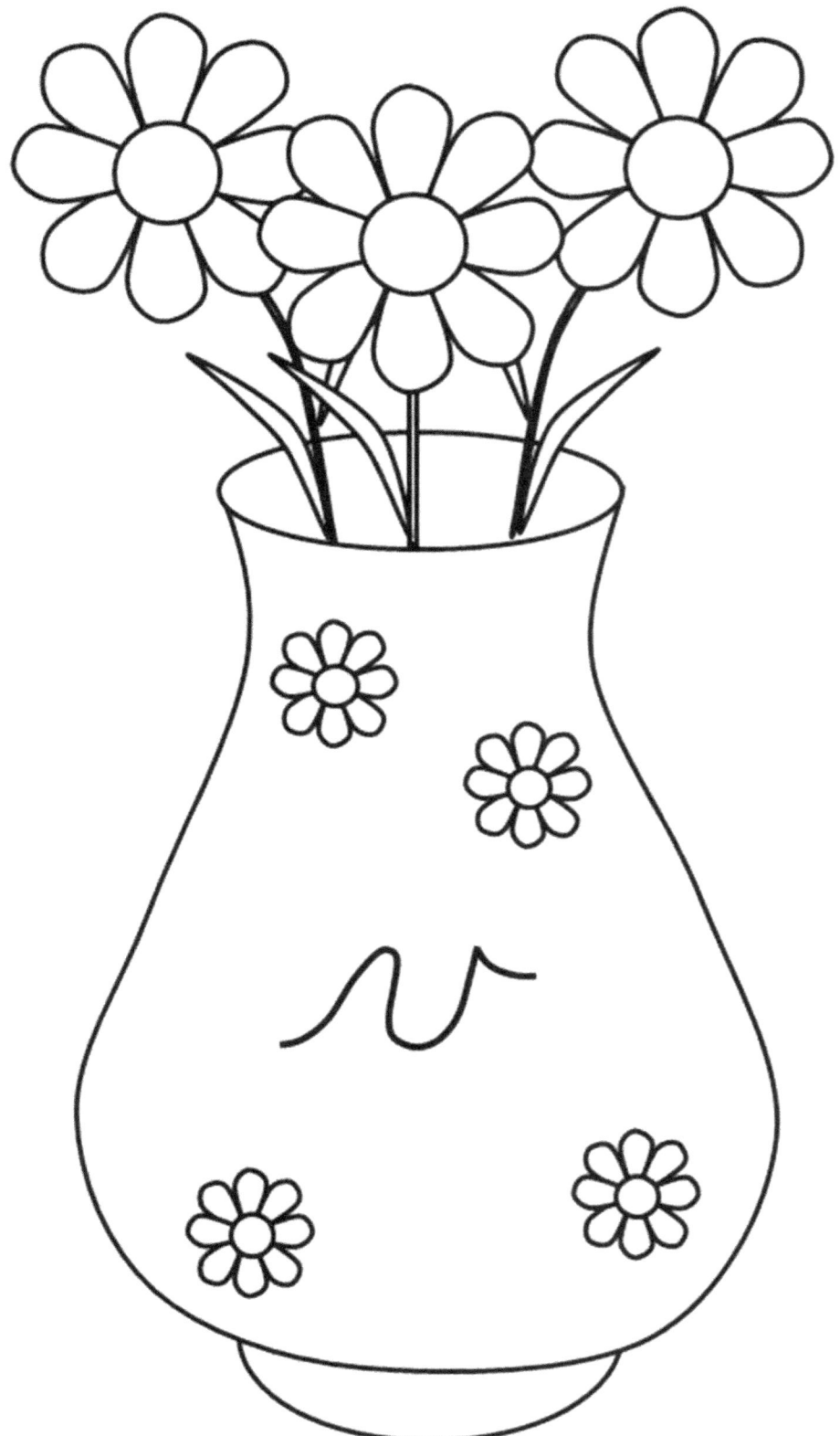

Trace the steps for making the letter v on the following line.

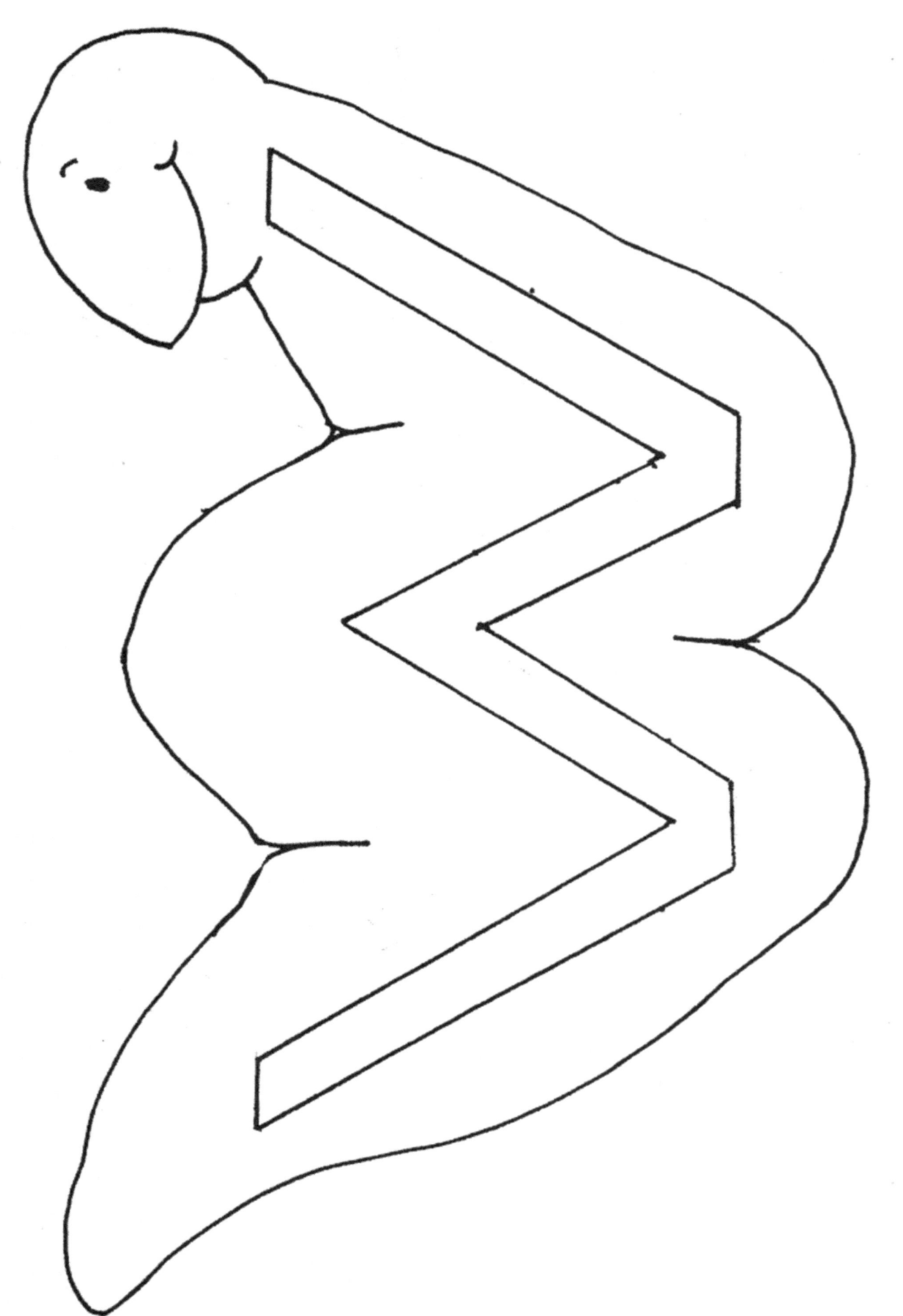

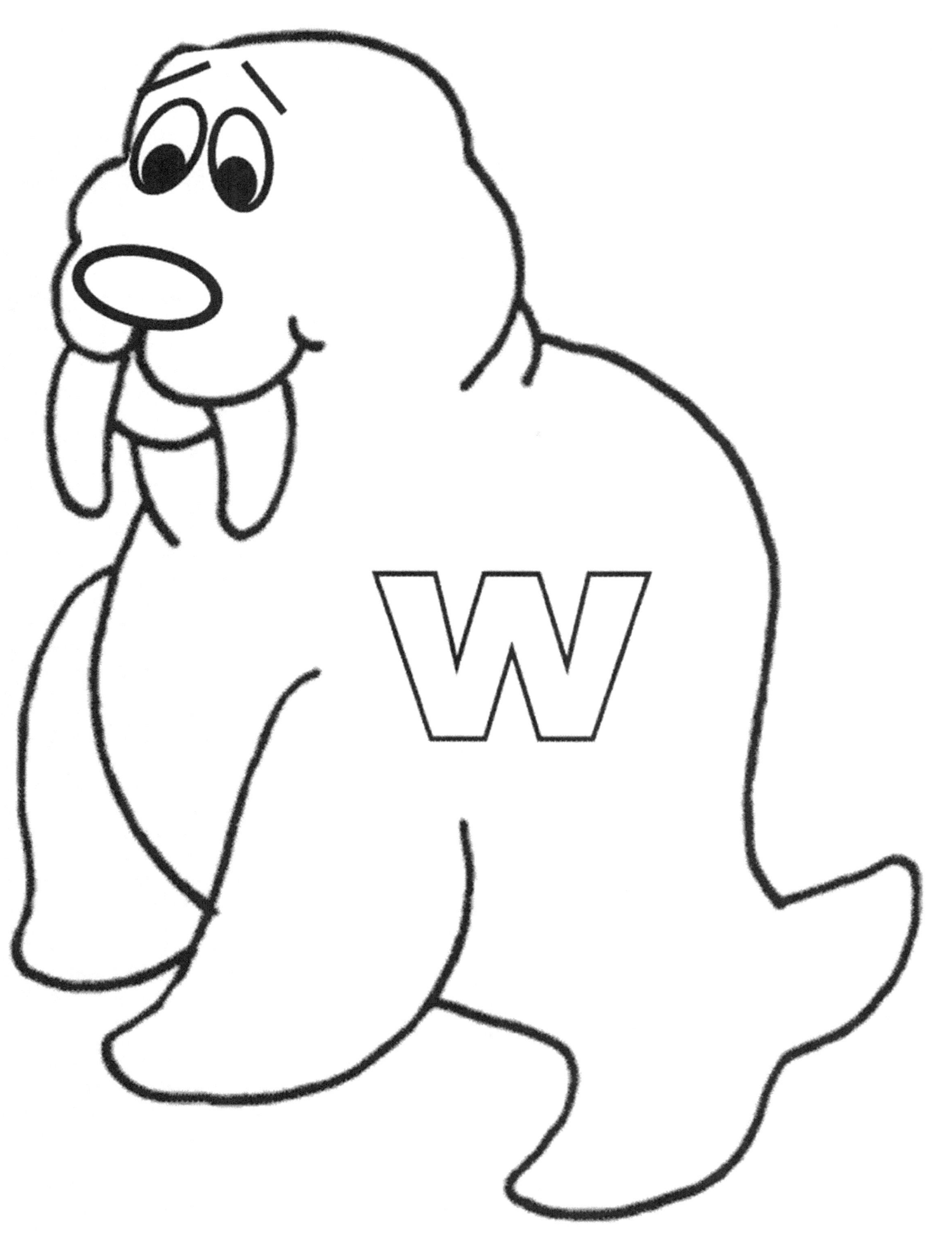

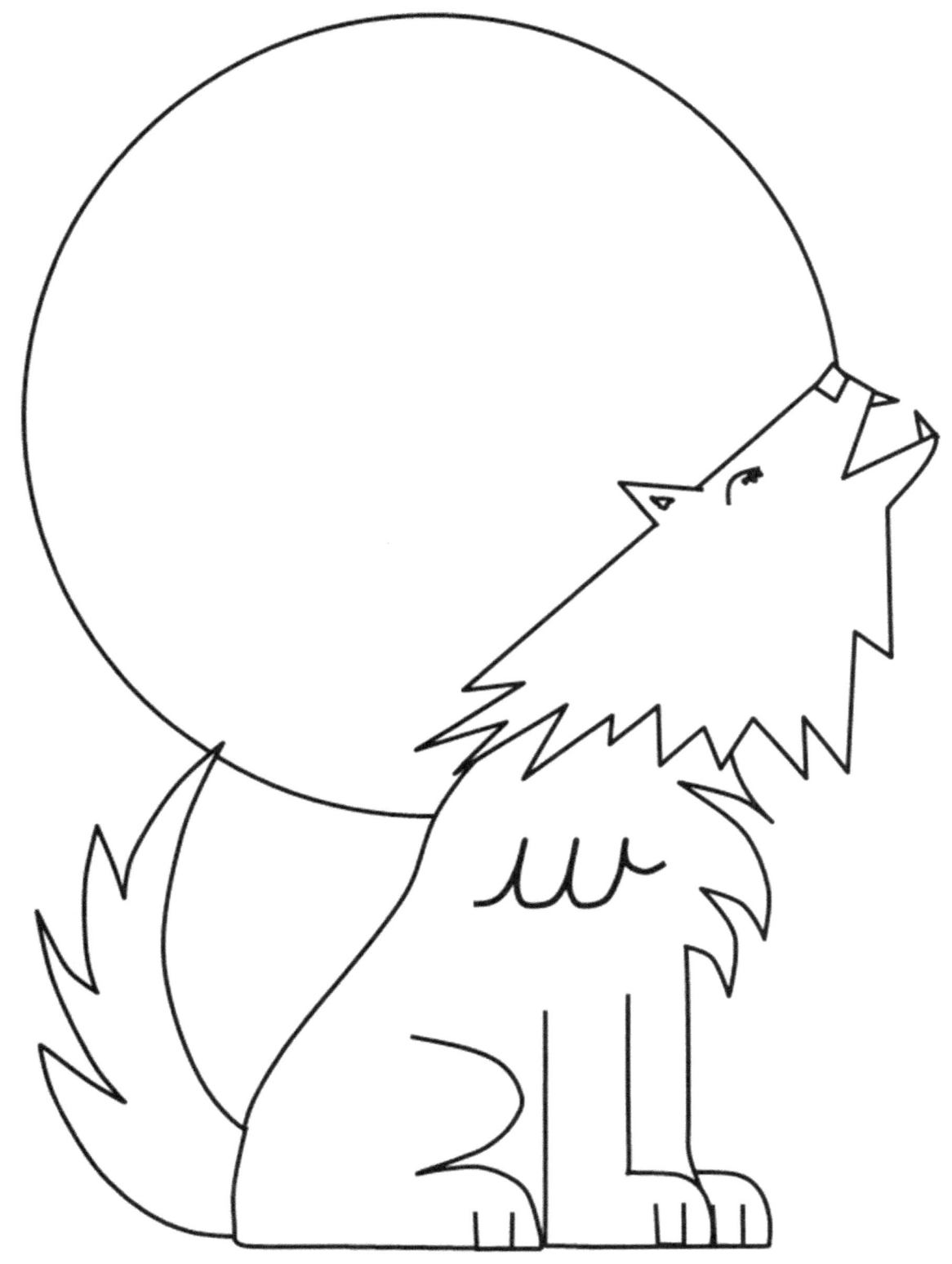

Trace the steps for making the letter w on the following line.

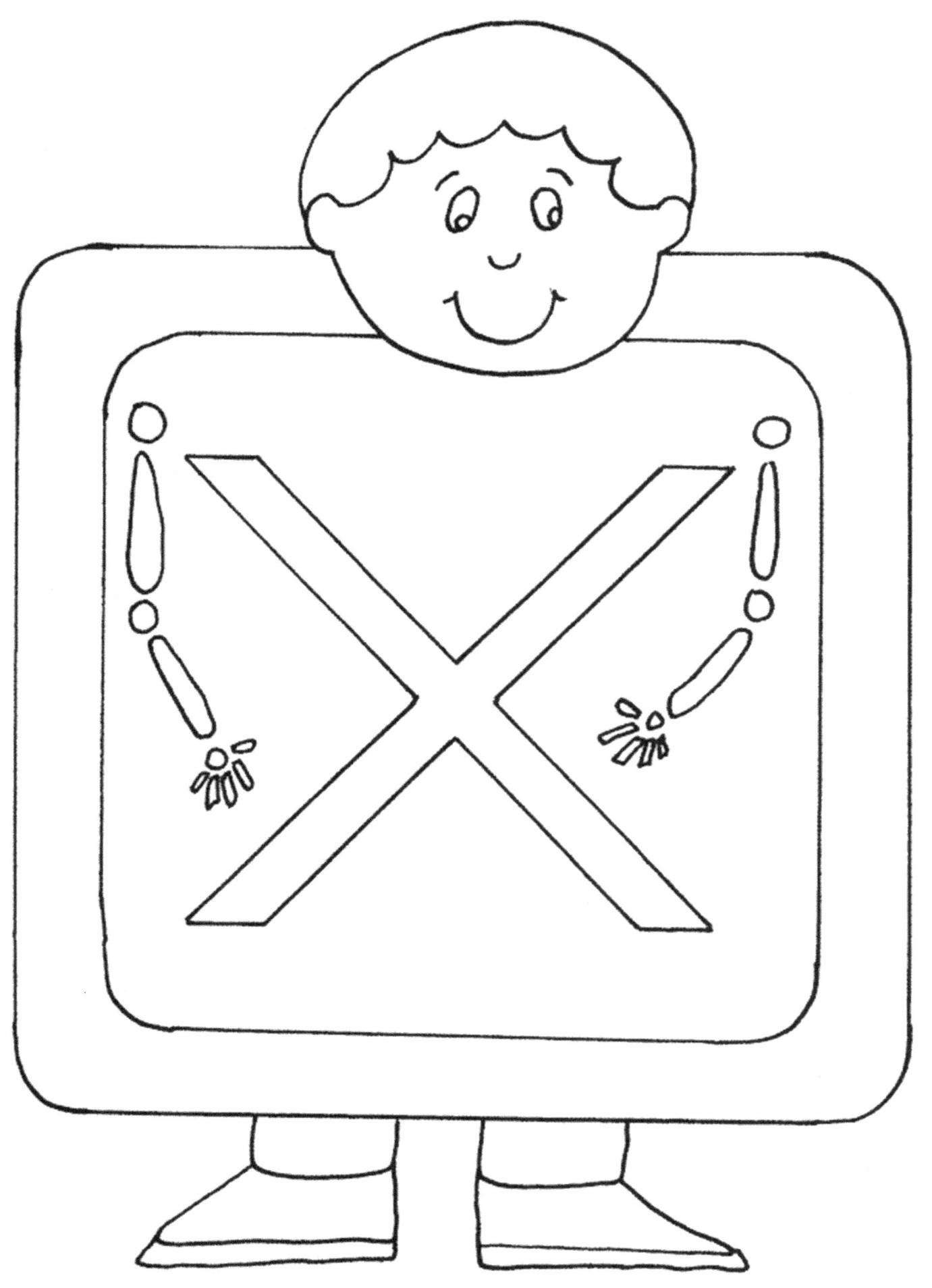

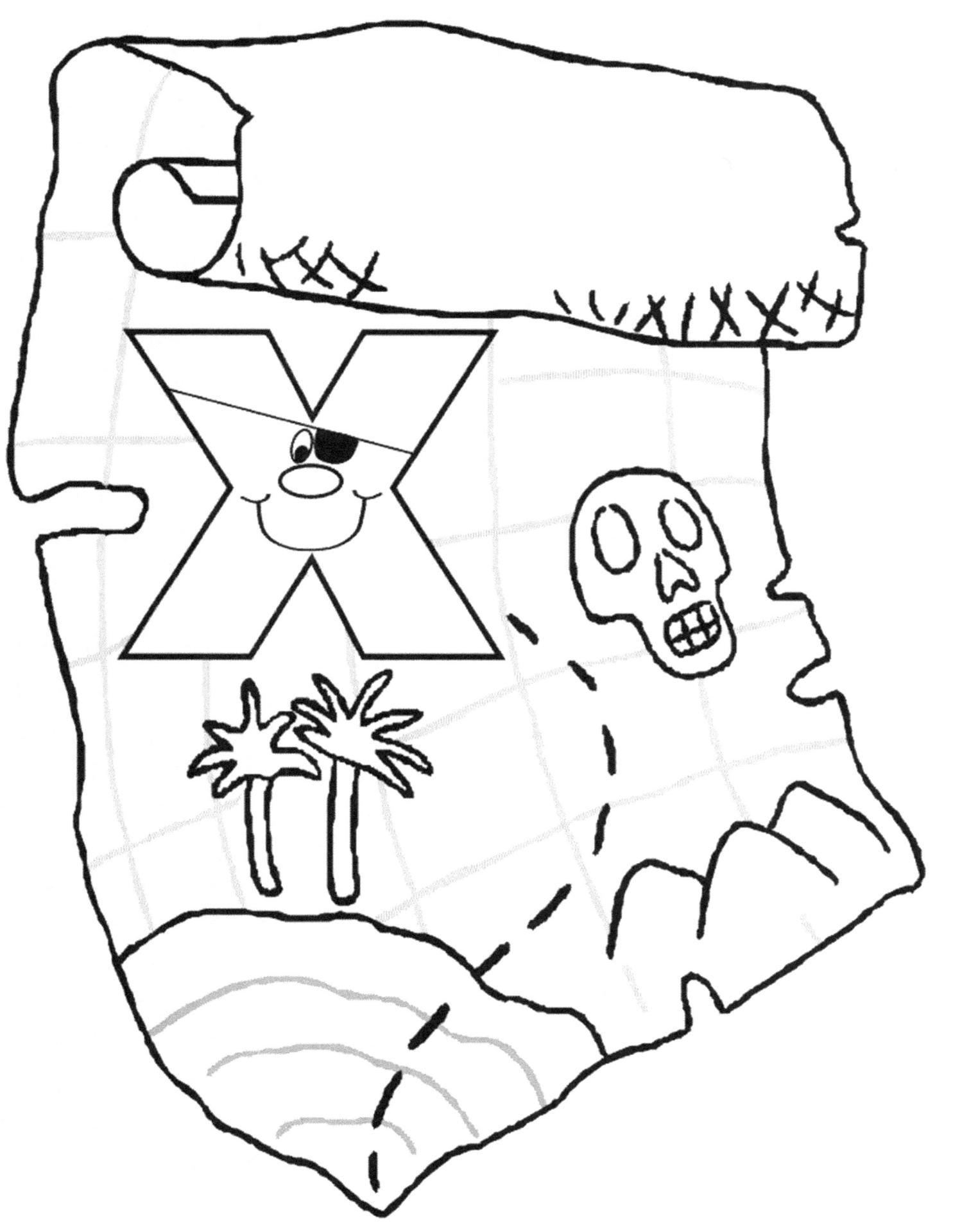

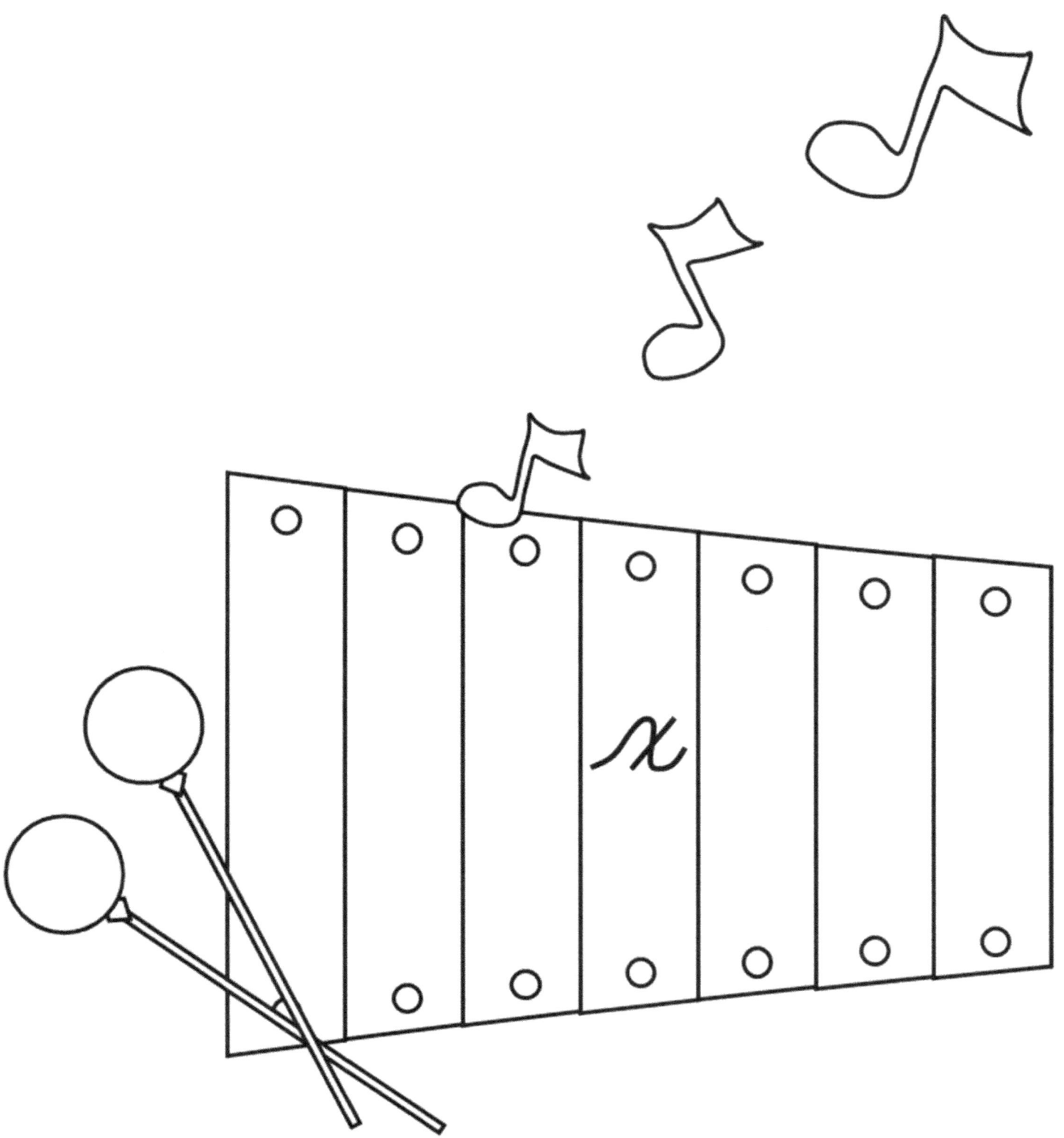

Trace the steps for making the letter x on the following line.

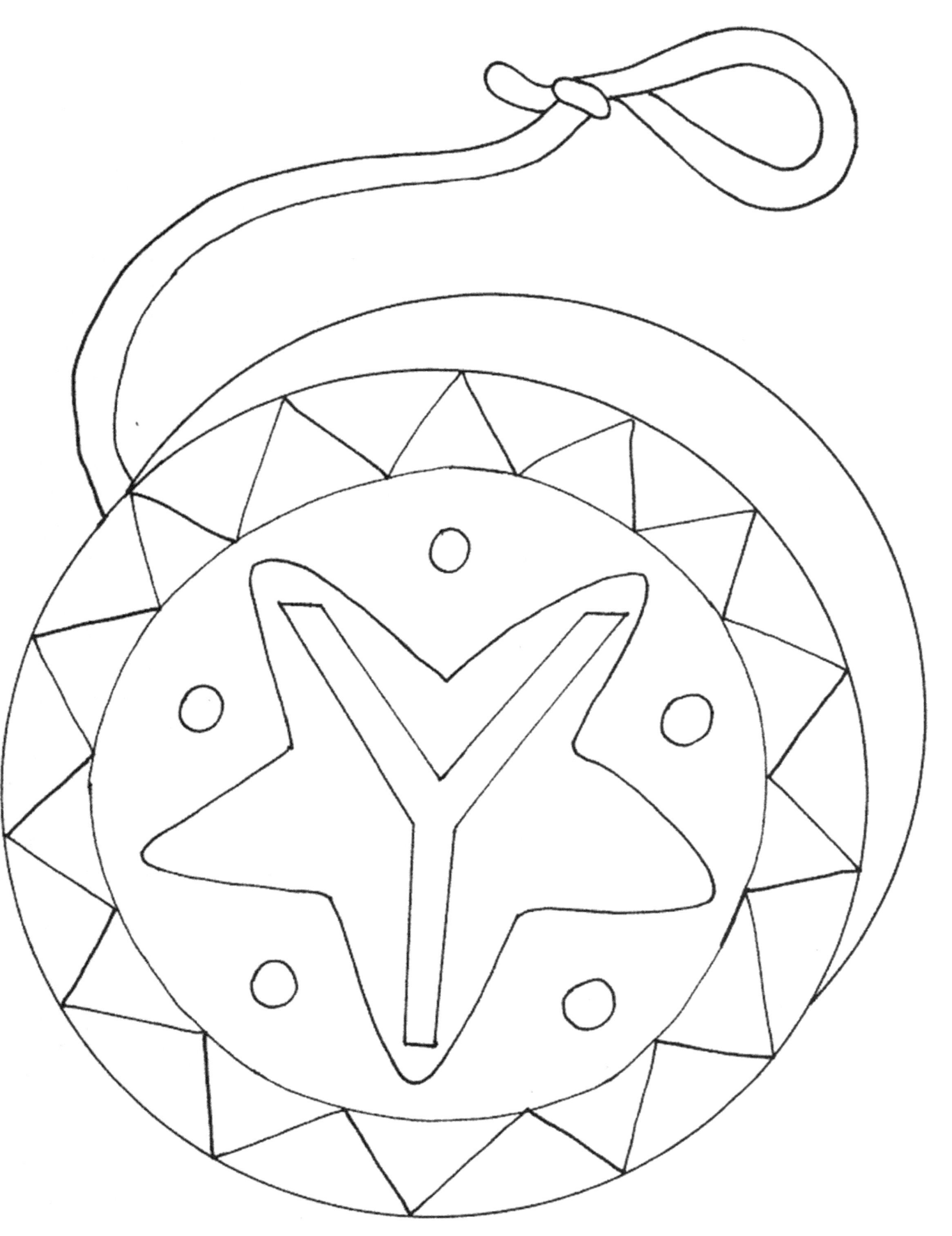

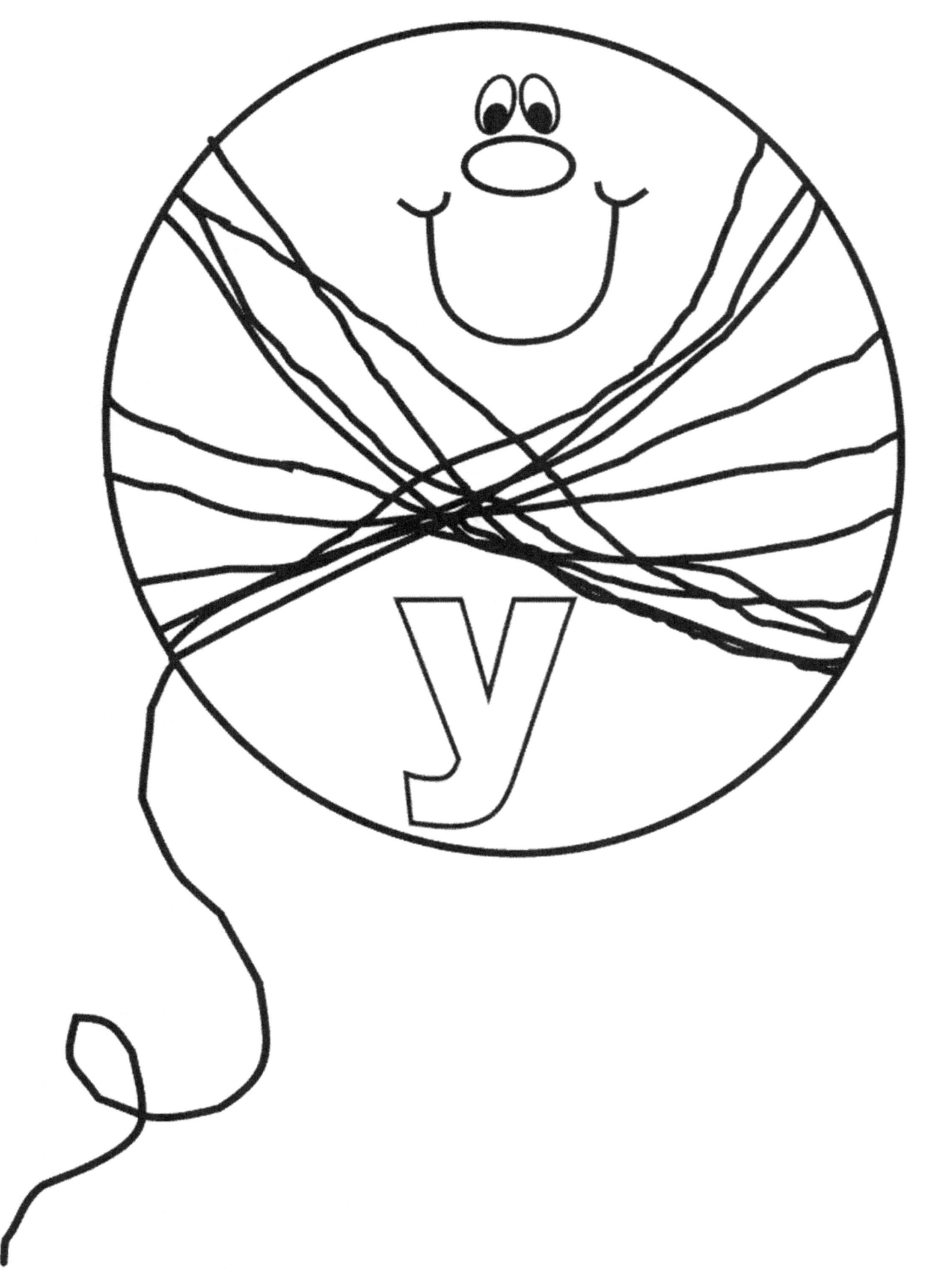

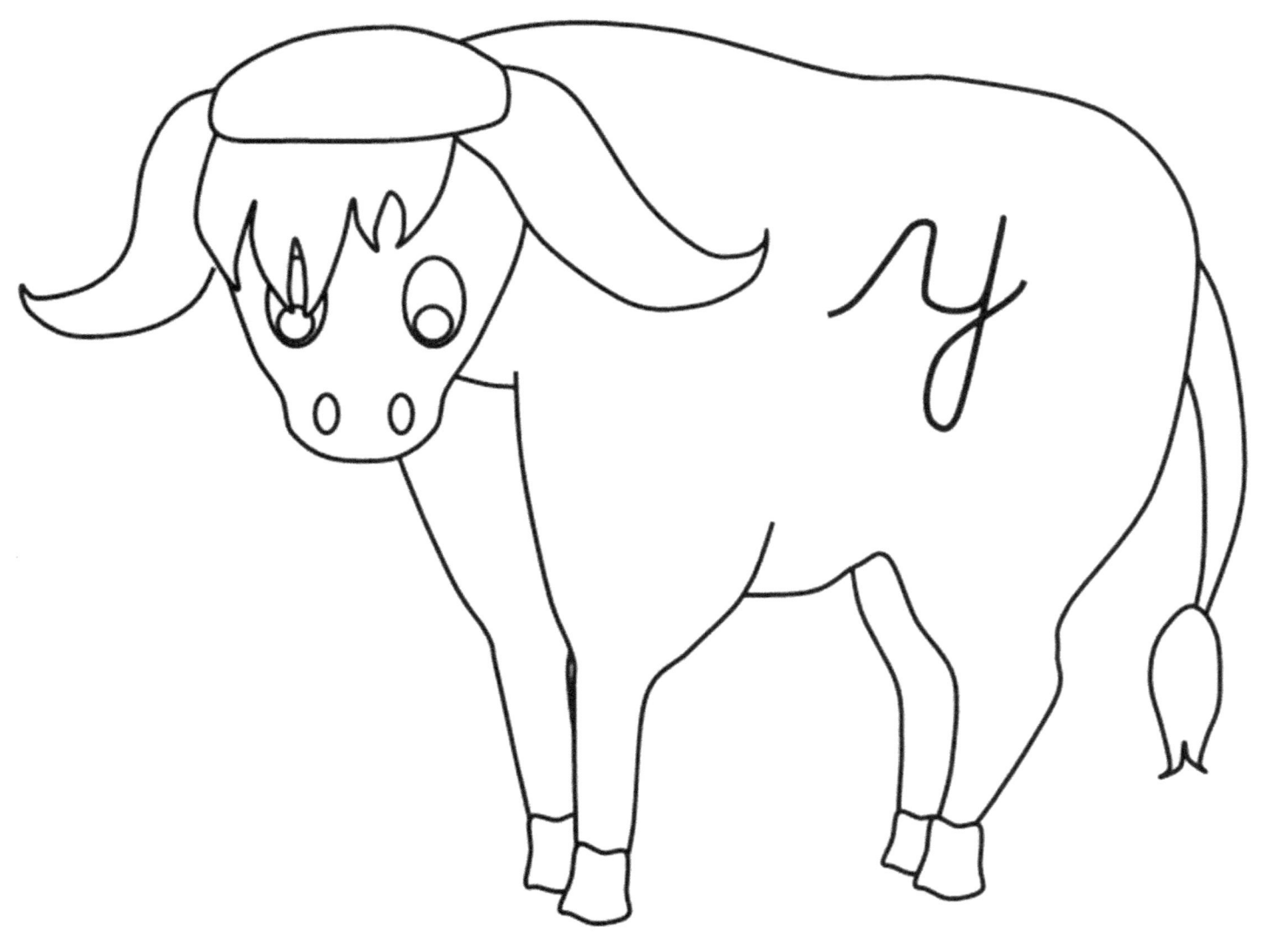

Trace the steps for making the letter y on the following line.

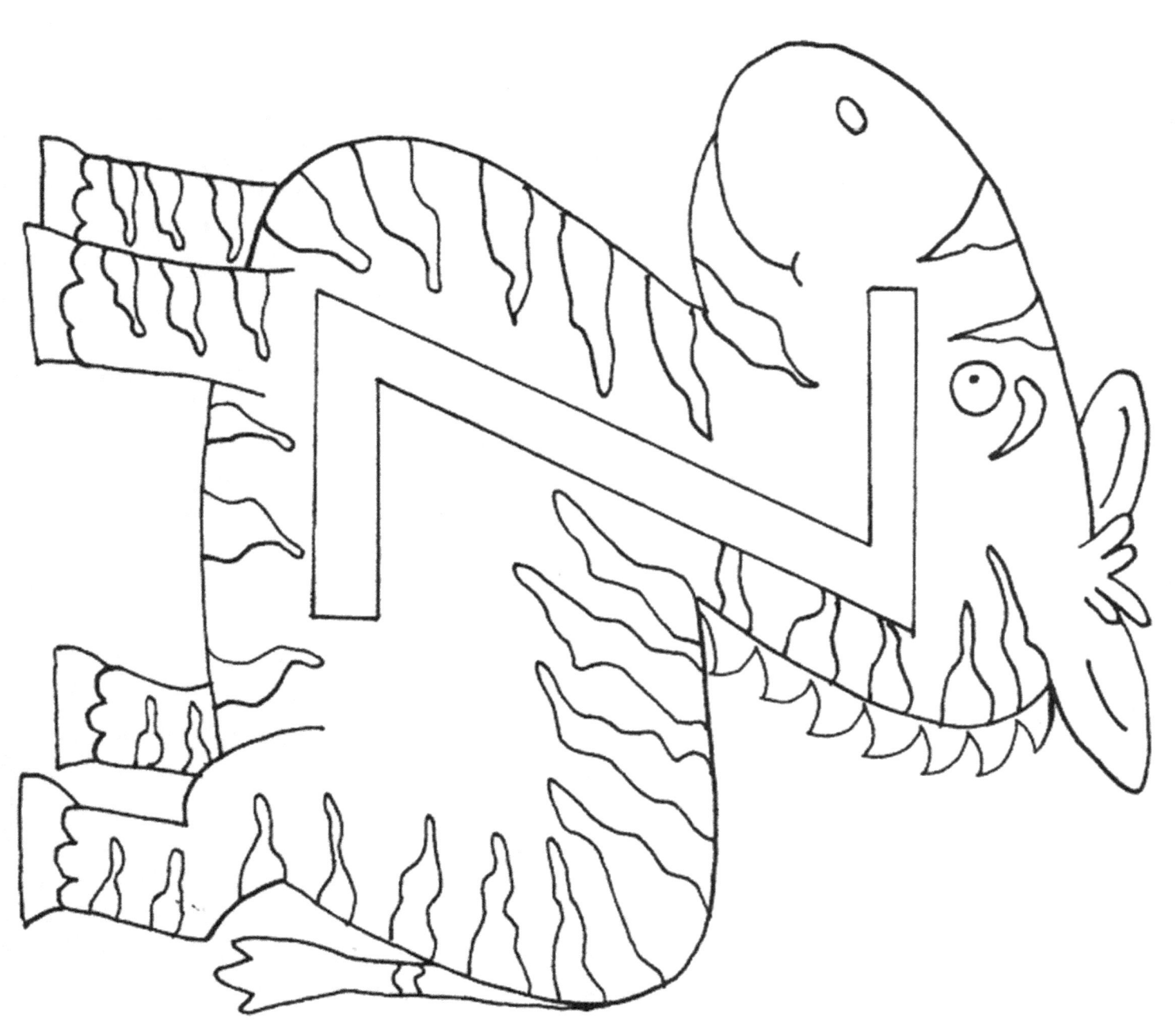

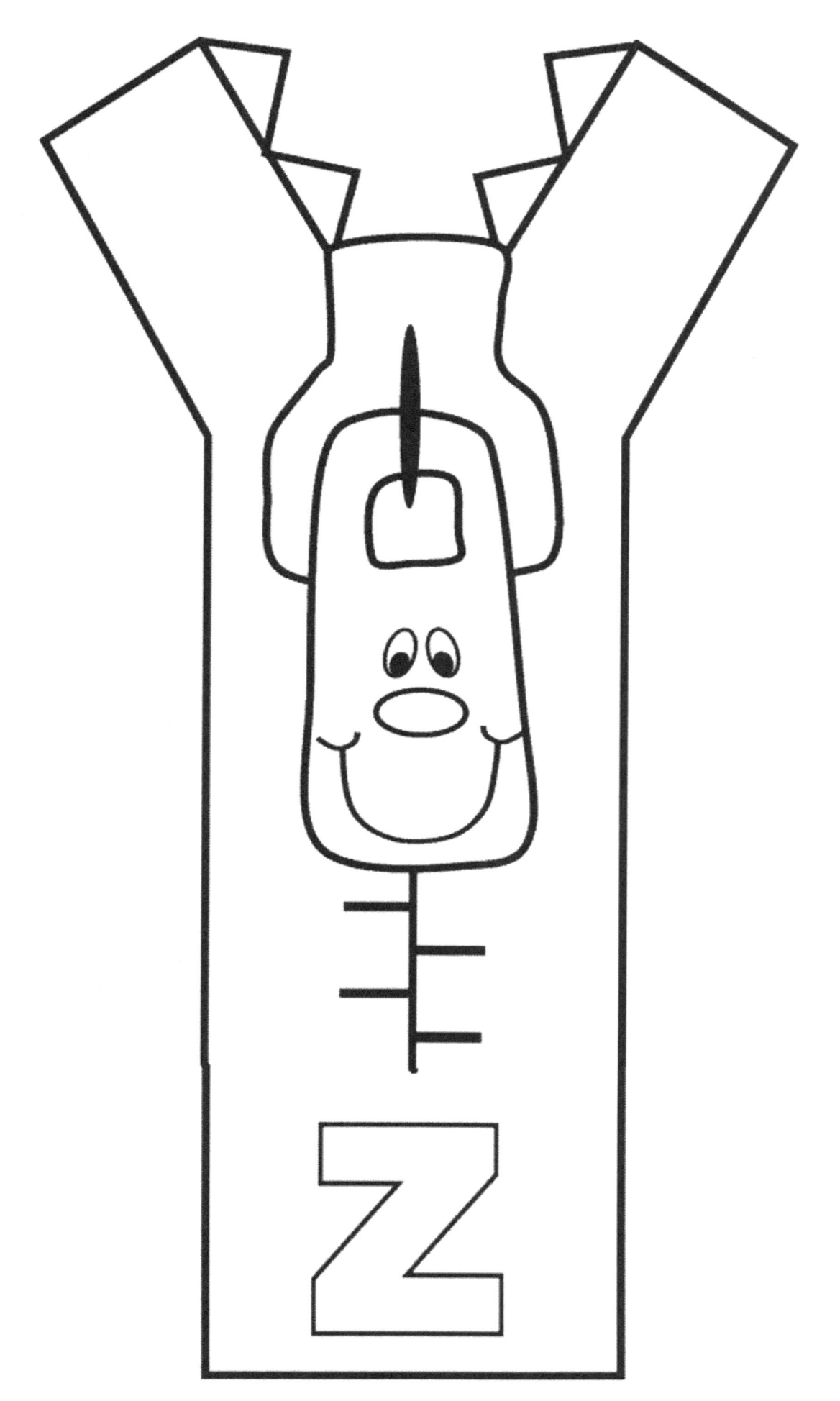

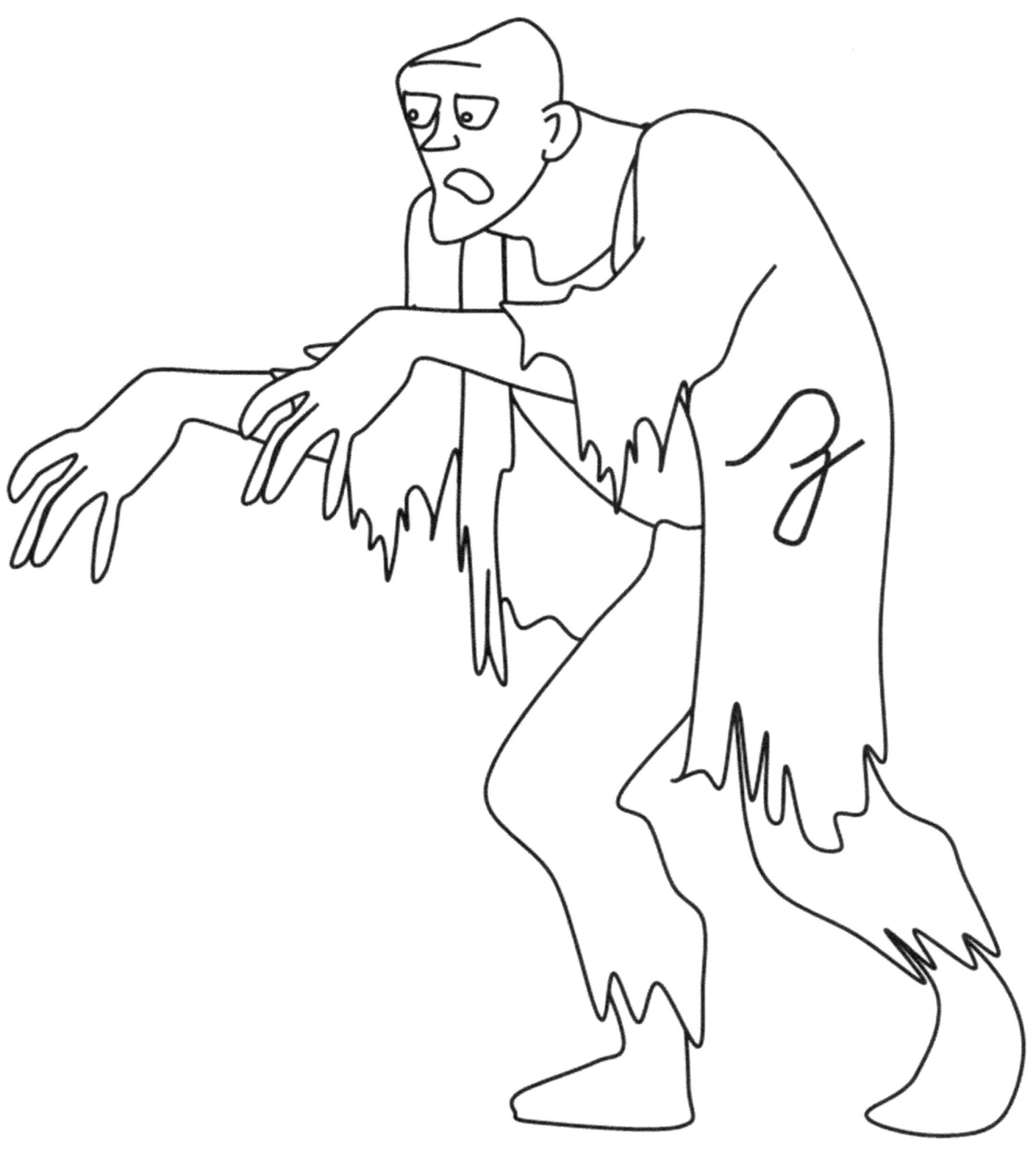

Trace the steps for making the letter z on the following line.